The PURPOSE *in the* PAIN

A Journey from Torment to Triumph

KAREN ROLAND-DOUGLASS

Mountain Ash
Press

Cover design by Stephanie Spino | Interior and ebook design by Skinner Book Services

DISCLAIMER: *The Purpose in the Pain* was written to aid people in self-discovery and personal growth through various strategies. The information here is provided for educational purposes only and is not intended as a substitute for working with a licensed healthcare professional and/or medical provider. The author assumes no legal liability for the results of actions taken regarding the use or non-use of this educational information. Client examples in this book have been modified to remove names and other identifying details to protect identities. They are included here to illustrate the concepts within the book. Please email all questions and concerns to gileadhealsministries@gileadheals.com.

See back matter for Scripture quoting permissions.

ISBNs: 979-8-9928149-0-3 (paperback)
       979-8-9928149-1-0 (ebook)

In loving memory
of your life and legacy, Mama
(Glady Poo)

A NOTE FROM THE AUTHOR

I dedicate this book to my mother, Gladys Anita Roland (1926–2020), who was my support and inspiration. She loved and saw me just as God made me uniquely and wonderfully in His image (Psalms 139). She demonstrated the courage and assurance to press on during immense pain, knowing there was purpose in the pain and that nothing could separate her from God's love.

In her Godly wisdom, my mother approached motherhood in a unique fashion. She loved each of her children in the unique way we needed to be loved. As a toddler, when I appeared unresponsive to sounds and voices, she took sign language classes to ensure she could communicate with me. She later realized nothing was wrong with my hearing – I didn't want to be bothered. I was her cautious and reflective child, and to ensure that her love for me was not overshadowed by Patricia, her firstborn, by Donald, her only son, and by Cecily, her social butterfly, she let it be known to all that I was "sweet as a rose in the middle of December." For those of you who do not know, yes, there is a rare and beautiful rose that blooms in December – the Christmas Rose.

Based on my personality, temperament, strengths, and fears, she understood that I needed to be her primary caregiver during the last year and a half of her life. She knew that I needed a head start on my grief to be able to live life on this side without her. I am forever grateful for the tears, laughter and memories that we shared and that she allowed me to care for her with the same devotion and unconditional love she showed me throughout my life.

To my siblings, Patricia, Donald (Andewnita), Cecily, and the world: my experiences and emotional and spiritual turmoil are not an indication of our mother or any others who impacted my life. I had a loving and kind mother and equally wonderful and supportive siblings, and there were many who spoke life into me, including you.

CONTENTS

Two natures beat within my breast.
The one is foul, the one is blessed.
The one I love, the one I hate.
The one I feed will dominate.

From *Crowded Skies: Letters
To Manhattan* by Tara Leigh Cobble

INTRODUCTION

"What is wrong with me?"

I know that you know this question well. It sneaks into your days especially when you find yourself aware that you are again facing the same problems again. It creeps behind the mask you are wearing, the one that keeps everyone else believing you are happy, successful, brave, and in control.

But you are so afraid that you will be found out, fearful that you will never be able to remove that mask. You have seen yourself in the mirror, and if you remove the mask, someone will see the woundedness that you see. They will not understand you and will judge you for what you have done or what has been done to you. You feel—in your chest, your stomach, your spirit—an uneasiness, and it is growing. Your grip over your circumstances is loosening, and it is only a matter of time

I

before you lose what control you have. You could ask for help, but you dare not take off your mask. You are trapped, feeling isolated and alone; you don't have anyone who will understand or anyone who you can trust with the broken pieces of your heart and your crushed spirit.

I know this and have seen it often. Laura, a patient of mine, came to see me when she was fifty-five. She was molested as a child; she was only ten when her mother's boyfriend's molestation occurred. It went on for about five years; she was afraid to say no. She did not tell anyone and took on the responsibility for her violation. She struggled for years, knowing in her adult mind that it was not her responsibility, but she continued to carry the shame and self-blame.

It is isolating to be in turmoil. It brings negative feelings like guilt and shame, and you hear the voices that spoke fear and shame into you. You are tired. You need to make a change.

Inner turmoil is conceived and birthed out of fear, pain, and self-doubt. It is rooted in confusion, trauma, despair, and chaos. Inner emotional turmoil is often camouflaged with a proud strut, pristine grooming, and an outwardly false sense of unshakable confidence, but on the inside, you are trapped in deep darkness. Voices from your past torment you despite what you have accomplished and what you have accumulated. Others tell you, *You are amazing, you are successful, you are beautiful*, but none of what they say could ever be true. You tell yourself, *They don't know me. They don't know my story.* Even though you manage to forget about it, on most days, you are haunted by what was said or done to you. You thought you could bury it deep inside of you and never visit the things that haunt you again. You did what they told you to do, you forgot about it, you acted as though it never happened, and you ignored the voices in your head that would repeat the horrifying things that people who should have loved you and protected you said. Now, you hear the echoes of the past, and you have lost the power to contain the pain. It is breaking forward in your consciousness. You are remembering bits and pieces of what happened, what they said and did to you. Although you are no longer the child who lived these experiences, you still emotionally feel helpless and deeply hurt as though you are that same child that did not have a voice and couldn't do anything about the things that were happening and the situations that you found yourself involved in. You are filled with anger and self-hatred. You blame yourself and you live in shame. You ask yourself why; you ask yourself what is wrong with you. You now tell yourself the horrible things that others said to the child within you. You have accepted the blame and taken on the responsibility for the actions of those that have hurt and caused you trauma.

You have been drawn to this book because you are at a place in your life where you are aware of the struggle that is deep within yourself. You are not quite sure what is causing the battle, but you have experienced the effects of it for many years and have managed to live with it. In some cases, you were even able to thrive despite it. However, the challenge and desire to live a fulfilled life will not allow you to ignore the turmoil that you have struggled through over the years. It has become unbearable. Yet, just as you know the intensity of your pain, you know that there is a place of healing and freedom, but you don't know where to find it and what it looks like. You have been in bondage for so long that you have forgotten yourself and who you were before the pain. You have forgotten when you were happy and free to be you. You can't even describe what you are feeling, but you can clearly see the effects of the pain of your past.

This book is a guide meant to assist you in your journey of finding inner peace and an understanding of the turmoil that grips your soul so tightly that you almost feel like you can't breathe. I want to walk with you in your desperate desire to be free, free from your past, free from the pain, free from the woundedness that shows up in your days.

Turmoil is a sense of intense emotional distress, confusion, or uncertainty. Turmoil manifests in feelings of anxiety, distress, insecurities, self-doubts, and negative mindsets (*I can't, I won't, I never will*). It is your inner child crying out to be seen, heard, and protected. It is your inner child fighting against what was said or done, or that which should not have been said or done, or what was not said or done at all. You have been looking for answers, wanting and longing to be loved and told how lovable you really are. Your inner child is searching to make sense of the self-hatred and doubt, yet you do not really know where it comes from and why it has such a strong pull.

The inner turmoil is occurring because what has protected you from the pain for all of these years is no longer effective. The once-strong defense mechanisms that served you and protected you for many years were like a newly constructed brick building. Over time, that building withstood the wind and the rain; it survived the storms of life. But lack of maintenance and attention over the years has caused the building to become dilapidated; the mortar has begun falling apart. If you walk past the building and brush against it, the mortar will fall to the ground. Your defenses protected your psyche from the pain of your past, but now the walls are flimsy and no longer serve their purpose. That is why you are becoming inundated with the pain of your past. It is time to rebuild on a new foundation and fortify yourself with strength that already lies deep within, the strength that you were born with before the pain. You must be reborn.

I am no novice when it comes to trauma, emotional hurt, and woundedness. In fact, my woundedness began in the womb. I arrived in the world as the fourth child born to a single mother already raising three children, ages four, seven, and nine, with no noteworthy help from their fathers. As far back as I can remember having a perception of self, I felt unwanted, invisible, and unloved. Whether or not this was true matters little; these thoughts, feelings, and preconceptions were real, and they became embedded into my emotional DNA. I believed my voice had no value; I stood in the shadows of others.

Even though I lived with this belief, there must have been something inside me fighting against it. In fact, when seniors in my high school were asked to state their life's motto, I selected mine from the song "The Greatest Love of All." I was not clear why I chose this song, but its message resonated in my heart and captured what was in the depths of my soul: Being in the shadows of someone else was not my destiny—I would find the self-love that lived inside of me.

Even so, I agreed to this belief for many years, and I lived in turmoil. The turmoil caused me to wear a mask for many years, and I hid behind it, hoping that no one would ever see who I thought I was, how broken and unlovable I believed myself to be. I hid the tears that I cried; I wore the mask to hide the pain that lay inside. The mask let me pretend I was someone who I did not know. It gave me permission to be what people wanted me to be.

The prenatal trauma, however, set me up to have an innate sensitivity to the emotional, psychological, and spiritual pain of others and gave me the desire to embrace and heal my own woundedness and to encourage, support, and guide others as they travel along their path of hope and healing. I was destined to help others heal from physical, emotional, psychological, and spiritual wounds. Today, as a clinical psychologist and spiritual facilitator for over thirty years, I meet with people from all walks of life who are living in bondage. They are pressed down with emotional and psychological hurt and pain that penetrates to the core of their souls. They are people trapped in their woundedness. Some of the people I meet want to remain in the prison of their pain due to fear that they will be overtaken by the intense pain and overwhelming emotions. Others will remain in the prison of their pain due to denial. I have come to see that only by examining the wounds will we become free.

This book is for you who has decided that you will no longer dismiss, ignore, or justify the pain. Instead, you would rather examine that place of woundedness. You need to understand the source of your turmoil and what forces are fueling it.

I am asking you, reader, to commit to the work of freeing your spirit from the chains that bind you to lies. It is difficult work, I know, because I have done it. What I learned was that the pain was not in what happened to me but in keeping up the pretense. Along the way, I had somehow agreed to a set of beliefs that told me who I was, and I agreed to perpetuate those beliefs.

I bring this book to you as a light. It is meant to illuminate you as you travel down your path of healing. I know it is terrifying not to know where the path will lead, and there are times when you will want to turn back, but there is freedom on the other side. The journey of healing and peace must first start in a place deep inside of you, in a place of silence and solitude. When you draw your mind, body, and spirit inward, the answers will come freely. You must start from the very beginning.

As you move into this book, I encourage you to meditate on the message of each chapter and to commit to the work that will bring you to freedom. As someone who turns to the church for healing and guidance, I do share stories and passages from the Bible that underscore the concepts of this book; I share them here in hopes that, whatever your beliefs and practices, you see their purpose and universal qualities.

At the end of each chapter is a series of reflective questions designed to help you move through the pain, from woundedness to freedom. I give you permission to use this space to write your responses. Take your time, and let your heart and spirit guide you to the answers. If the work is painful, be forgiving of yourself and give yourself time to care for your needs. What you awaken in your questioning may be difficult to face—after all, we don't want to see how we participated in our pain—but it is necessary to face the truth. This personal work can be intense. I also give you permission to put the book down and regroup as you need.

As you move towards an understanding of the lies that have entrapped you in a life you do not want, you will begin to feel lighter. But beware—what is painful also can be comforting in its familiarity. It is easy to turn back to your habits, to the safety of routines, and to the people who validate the life you live now. You know your spirit needs to soar, and you will need to lift away from the life you have now. You will need to commit yourself to a new vision of yourself and your life, where you can live with peace and ease. To place accountability on those to whom it belongs and to embrace self-forgiveness and extend forgiveness to the perpetrators without removing the accountability. To dig deep within and identify the lies that were once told and that were self-perpetuated and replace them with the truth of the greatness of who you are. To facilitate healing of the wounded heart and spirit and find the purpose of the pain as we walk in divine destiny.

What I do know is this: You are able to face the trauma and the pain that you have borne for many years, you can forgive those who inflicted that pain, and you can forgive yourself for perpetuating the pain. You can make sense of the chaos and struggle you have endured. You can find self-love where there is self-hatred. Self-doubt and shame do not belong to your spirit. You can find the purpose in the pain you have lived with so intimately.

You must only believe freedom is worth it.

As you read this book you will embark on an emotional and spiritual journey of self-love, awareness, acceptance, and healing. You will courageously face past trauma and pain that has caused deep seeded emotional and psychological wounds. You will challenge the lies that were told to you so repeatedly that they became internalized. Do not be afraid; you are not alone; the strongest part of you is in you already. As we read in 2 Timothy 1:7, "For God has not given us a spirit of fear but of power and of love and of a sound mind" (NKJV).

You will realize that you are not who you have become; you are not what happened to you; you are not to blame or be ashamed of what happened to you; you are not what they called you; you are not invisible; you do not have a voice that is not worth being heard; you are not unworthy, unlovable, or inferior. You will be delivered from people, relationships, circumstances and those internal voices from your past that keep you trapped in your pain and woundedness. You will clearly recognize the purpose in the pain. You will confidently walk out your divine purpose, knowing that you are uniquely and wonderfully made.

Chapter 1

THE TURMOIL FROM WITHIN

The flames will not consume you.
—Isaiah 43:2 (NLT)

I felt trapped—as though I was being interrogated by a police officer. Each time I responded, another question followed. It might sound dramatic, but at that moment, I could understand how, over time, suspects would shut down and just give the answers that the interrogator is looking for.

"You don't want people to walk into our house whenever they want, do you?" my husband says to me.

"I am not talking about giving the code out. It will just be easier to get in if you forget your key."

My husband and I are talking about a keyless door

entry pad. I want one. He wants me to convince him we need one.

"Why do you want it, though?" he insists.

My words are becoming short. "I'm just asking because we talked about it and never got one."

"But why do you want it?" he asks again.

It is such a mundane conversation, the kind that all spouses have, but my mind is reacting as though there is more at stake. He is interrogating me, and I am trapped in a place where I have to justify my feelings and reasons for wanting something as simple as an entry pad. *Don't I have a right to want it? Don't I have a right to have a voice, an opinion?*

I am quickly pulled into that place in my body where I feel I am expected to be invisible, seen but not heard.

No, no, no. I refuse to be invisible. There she is, the part of me who wants to be heard, who wants to be seen, the advocate. I push aside the other side of me, the shrinking violet, the part of me who agrees to take her place in the familiar place of silence when someone questions me. Old wounds are punctured, and the bleeding starts again as if it is a fresh wound. The bleeding is so profuse that my sense of healing and well-being is in a critical state. Although it was a minor issue in the scheme of things for me, it was crucial. Did I shut down, become engulfed in sadness, and relive all the times I did not have a voice, or did I stand my ground and fight for my voice to be heard? I decided at that moment to fight.

I expressed my desire in a firm voice, expressed that I had nothing else to say, and required that he tell me why he was against it. I felt empowered and realized that I could become the integrator if I realized that I have a voice, and it is a powerful voice.

Our quick exchange that day took me to a place where I felt my voice wasn't important. I didn't want to justify my opinion. Later, I realized it was not the keyless entry pad that was triggering this; it was my husband questioning me. It triggered a lot of unresolved feelings. I was not being dramatic—my woundedness had an impact on my present life. Within moments, once again, I was standing in my sister's shadow, the youngest of four children. I felt unimportant. *Why can't I just have an opinion?* My inner advocate asks. *Why can't I be seen for who I am?*

My husband just wanted an explanation, but it brought up my unresolved fears.

In childhood, I felt like an invisible child. I was deeply sensitive, but in my heart and mind, I had no voice. I felt like I did not exist in the outside world, so insignificant that no one could see me even if they tried. But I wanted to be seen, I wanted to be heard, I wanted to be valued. As I grew, so did the internal battle within me. *I do have a voice*, my advocate would insist, *I do have something to say. I want to be seen. I want to be heard.*

Then, my other side would return. *No, what you believe doesn't matter. No one hears you; no one cares.*

If I spoke up, there would be consequences. *You will be rejected*, the wounded child told me, *dismissed and taunted. It is not safe. Please don't. Just be quiet.*

It was a constant battle.

So many of us are living with inner turmoil. When we are wounded children, we grow up to be wounded adults. We learn to hide our guilt, shame, and pain. We learn to put on a mask to protect ourselves, and we dare not remove it for fear others will see the broken-ness-woundedness we see.

The rest of the world can't see our pain. They see us managing our lives, successfully balancing the demands of work and home. They see our accomplishments and our achievements. They see us laughing and smiling.

They don't see the wounds. They don't see how we, the wounded, spend our days working to prove our success is deserved. No matter how much we have accomplished, we are always waiting for something to go wrong. Some of us work so hard to reach our goals that we find out the rewards are not really all that fulfilling in the end. There is emptiness where there should be wholeness.

In my working life, I am a licensed clinical psychologist and spiritual facilitator. Many people cross my path in my work, and I recognize the wounded. They arrive knowing they need to fix something in their lives. They have been trying to fix it for a long time. They are moving in this world aimlessly, doing what they have done in the past, whether it is moving from relationship to relationship or engaging in risky behavior—drinking, gambling—and they are trying to escape what they are feeling. Sometimes they know what is causing their pain; sometimes they do not.

Many of us know this inner turmoil well. We don't need an appointment with a therapist or a diagnosis. Even so, let us talk about it. Turmoil is a great disturbance in your sense of peace, and it creates confusion, a distressing uncertainty of who you are and what your purpose is in this life. It is an inner battle between how you are perceived—by yourself and by others—and who you know you are really born to be. You can't seem to reconcile the two, and you live your life in pieces. You might even feel like the nursery rhyme character Humpty Dumpty, who had a great fall. All the kings, horses, and all the king's men can't put Humpty together again.

We don't need our lives to be falling apart to understand turmoil. From the outside, we appear to be doing fine. But if you are here with me, reading these words, you know as well as I do, that inner turmoil is a disruptor. It overtakes us in mundane moments, on the sunniest of days and in the middle of celebrations. It finds us, and it disrupts our lives.

We are wounded. We know this turmoil, and we want

to be free of it. Many of us try to outrun the turmoil because if we stop and face it, we need to embrace difficult feelings. In moments, we will be overtaken by feelings of fear, shame, powerlessness, inadequacy, or other equally powerful negative emotions. The desire to be free is in battle with the fear of being overtaken.

We try to outrun turmoil, but in doing so, we veer off on paths that lead us back to the same place we started.

It is painful to live with inner turmoil, isn't it? There is anguish when you long for self-understanding and awareness but cannot find it; when you never really feel adequate or accepted; when you are surrounded by friends but remain closed off to any real intimacy; when you are told you are too sensitive. It is lonely to be fiercely independent because you learned early on in life that if you do not care for yourself, no one will. Some of us stay up at night trying to figure out how to respond to situations; we are never sure of ourselves.

We feel caged. We feel stuck. We are emotionally and spiritually fatigued.

There are good reasons for our woundedness. Some of us were physically and sexually abused as children. Some of us were abandoned by our mothers or fathers or both. Some of us were raised by emotionally distant, cold, and even cruel parents or caregivers. Some of us lived in poverty and were left to fend for ourselves. Some of us were exposed to adult-like things when we shouldn't have been. Some of us have been in abusive relationships, where we were humiliated, demeaned, and bullied. Some of us have been betrayed, abandoned, and traumatized. The only way we can survive is to push the pain into the deepest recesses of our minds. But that woundedness remains, and it disrupts our lives.

I see people who are keenly self-aware and conscious of their struggle and its source. Others cross my threshold with a subconscious or unconscious awareness. They know something is disrupting their lives, but they don't understand why they feel like they do.

What painful things happened to you as a child or other significant developmental times in your life? Where are you in your awareness of those experiences and your reaction to them?

Use this space to record your thoughts.

_____

_____   _____

_____

_____

_____

_____

I often seek solace in church in my spiritual journey of enlightenment. It has allowed me to look inward, to explore the depth of my pain and embrace the feelings, and to attribute the callous acts that harmed me to whom they belong. The work I have done in this spiritual space has helped me illuminate my authentic self. I realized that the trials of this life blinded me to who I was created to be and my divine purpose and destiny. I understood that the words spoken over me do not define me unless I agree with them. I am worthy, I am loved, I am important, I am fearfully and wonderfully made. Anything outside of this is lies that are meant to keep me in bondage.

When I think of the inner turmoil some of us experience, I often think of the double-minded man described in the Bible. In the Book of James, we read: "He is a double-minded man, unstable in all his ways" (James 1:8 ESV). In this passage, we learn about a man who has two masters. He wants to be committed to his vision of himself as God sees him, but he is being pulled away from it. The spiritual conflict described in this passage echoes the struggle I see many of us grappling with. We are reminded that we must dedicate ourselves to one path. When our focus is divided, there is a lot of instability in our lives. We are in constant struggle, wanting to be free of what harms us or holds us back but unsure of how to become free. The strain we experience reveals itself in our behaviors and in our thoughts.

What I am here to tell you is this: Yes, you have been wounded. These emotional and psychological wounds that we experienced have penetrated the core of our souls. But we need to let go of the false beliefs that were ingrained in us. We need to become single-minded in our pursuit of freedom.

Some of us remain trapped in the prison of our pain for fear of being rejected. Others remain in denial and remain trapped for fear that we will be overtaken by the intense and overwhelming emotion of shame and worry, and we will have to bear all of the blame. Yet, if left untreated, our wounds can become infected.

The infection can spread to our lives and our relationships.

My niece is bright and talented, but I am certain she has never truly felt part of the family. That is easily explainable: For most of her life, she was raised by a couple who had no children. They were family friends. I didn't understand her connection to my family for many years until I learned that Lisa is my sister's daughter. She was never fully acknowledged as such. I finally discovered the truth in my early teens.

The circumstances of Lisa's conception had proved to be difficult for my sister. Patricia had been raped by one of her classmate's uncles. She was thirteen at the time. When Lisa was born, she was immediately taken away, and Patricia was sent to live out of state with our great-aunt. Patrica did not know what happened to Lisa for some years, and she was told not to talk about it, to act like she was never raped or had never given birth. There was never an opportunity for mother-child bonding.

Patricia did not have a say in the matter, and my mother accepted the counsel of her older aunts; the elders of the family did what they thought was best for everyone. Lisa is only six years younger than me, and I have watched her struggle with relationships and a sense of belonging. I suspect she struggles with her identity. Who is she? Who does she belong to? Did she ever feel that she really belonged to either family? I often wonder, if the circumstances had been different, what undiscovered potential would have replaced her struggles? It is unfortunate that my sister cannot help her in healing because she experienced such a great trauma and was not yet physically or emotionally equipped to handle its consequences herself as a young mother.

I remember a time when my family gathered at the home of an acquaintance. Patricia had not yet personally reckoned with her relationship to Lisa despite the presence of my niece in our lives. Her struggle with this relationship was unspoken, but it became visible that day.

After we arrived, the mother of Patricia's boyfriend exchanged pleasantries with us. She recognized me, my other sister Cecily, and my mother, and being polite, she asked for an introduction to Lisa.

"Who is this young lady?" she asked.

My sister must have been taken by surprise. "Oh," she said, "she's, my cousin."

The conversation continued, but I witnessed my niece visibly shrink. She knew who her birth mother was by now, but my sister could not speak the truth aloud. The lie hung in the air, invisible to the host but clearly visible to Lisa.

I know that shrinking feeling, and at that moment, I was returned to my childhood, to a day when a grown man loudly berated me.

Cecily and I were visiting her father's home, and we were all sitting at the dining room table. A friend of my sister's father. Whom I did not know by name and had never seen announced, "Oh, there is your father."

Both Cecily and I turned to look.

The man said, "I am not talking to you." His tone was stern and dismissive, even cruel. He tapped into my feelings of not being seen or wanted and being merely tolerated. Because of this his words seem to cut deep into my psyche.

I was hurt. Suddenly, I was floating in the air. I felt alone, detached from the people there, discarded.

I shrunk that day, much as I saw my niece shrink when her birth mother didn't acknowledge her. His words confirmed my burgeoning belief that I was not worthy of my space in the world. That was the moment when I felt thrown into Cecily's shadow. I was tolerated but not wanted.

These are the moments that do something to you, they? They have happened to many of us. You can probably pull up that feeling right now, the moment when you wonder, *why would someone do that to me? Why would they say that to me? Is something wrong with me?*

Our wounds are many, and we must seek freedom from their dominance over our spirits.

Here is what I know and what I have seen in my therapeutic practice. Yes, you experienced what you experienced, and I experienced what I experienced, but there are lies attached to those experiences. My sister believed she would be safer if she did not acknowledge her daughter, and I believed I had nothing to offer if I spoke up.

In my practice, I see how the lies we believe bleed into our lives. The young girl who is robbed of her innocence through sexual abuse believes she has no right to take control of her own body. She begins to equate her self-worth in terms of her sexuality. She is hurt again when she is called promiscuous. She has difficulty with trust; she says she desires intimacy, yet she sabotages any loving relationship. Sometimes, she is drawn to abusive and unhealthy relationships. She confuses love with emotional pain, so the greater the pain, the greater the love. As her body changes to a woman's frame, she becomes morbidly obese, hoping to ward off any advances and attention from men.

That is one story, but there are countless versions.

Steven is a young boy who is always hungry. He grows up feeling there is not enough for him. If he speaks aloud about his hunger at school, it brings unwanted attention to his home. Well-meaning social workers and teachers will pull Steven out of class to question him, but nothing will change. After years of neglect at home and no meaningful actions from others, he begins to believe he is not deserving of security. There is not enough to go around—not enough food, not enough of the good life—so he might as well get used to it.

But he wants it. As an adult now, despite his good job and financial security, Steven finds himself constantly comparing himself to his friends, wanting their ease in lifestyle. He can afford it now. He can fill his fridge, he can buy the car he wants, he can get tickets to any concert. He can have comfort and ease, but the lie is too strong. *There's not enough for me, so why take the risk?* His business is stagnant because he will not invest in its growth—if he takes that financial risk, it may not pay off, and then what? Some people just don't get to have it all.

When I talk to him, it's clear Steven does not see the skills and strengths he has gained from surviving poverty. Instead, he remains true to the lie: there is not enough for him, and he is not good enough to deserve it. Do not speak of it; it will only bring eyes to you.

In my practice, I see lies like this do long-term harm. The girl-child who was abandoned or rejected by a parent develops feelings of being unworthy and unlovable. She wonders why her parents are not around when all of her friends' parents are there. She spends a lot of time wondering what she did wrong and how to make her parents love her. Her little girl's beliefs remain as she grows, and she spends years trying to fill the emotional void that only the missing parent can fill. However, she is now an adult and no longer needs the type of love a parent offers a child. The opportunity has been lost, but she continues to seek that love, often looking for it in partners who are not emotionally or physically available, reinforcing her feeling that she is unlovable.

Our deficit tends to become our desire. We internalize the harm and connect it to our value, and it becomes part of our pain. This is how we attach lies to our experience.

I carry lies, too. Mine rest in the part of me that shrinks back when questioned, in the place that still asks for reassurance that I am, in fact, loved and not tolerated. I was born to a single mother who already had three children. Early in her life, knowing her mother did not want her—the pain of being separated from her mother told her so—my mother made a promise to herself that she would never give up the care of her children to anyone else. Imagine the turmoil of keeping a childhood promise like that, knowing that you are barely able to provide for and nurture the three you already have, knowing that the father of the child in your womb has already turned his back on both of you. I was born into a moment where my mother was struggling to take care of a fourth child and battling her own internal feelings of inadequacy, worthlessness, and being unloved. It turned out my mother was exceptional, but I believe her pain was passed on and perpetuated in the beliefs I developed. I felt *tolerated* and did not believe I had a right to my voice. I was afraid, on guard, waiting in anticipation for something terrible to happen.

Sometimes, trauma seeps out of our being, and we don't know where it comes from. We don't need to know where the lie comes from to know we are wounded. When I was young, six or seven years old, whenever there was a storm, as the sky darkened and the rain beat upon the windowpanes, I would sit on the couch fully dressed in my blue-and-white houndstooth coat, holding onto one of my mother's old purses, where I hid some pennies. I sat like that, waiting for my mother to get home safely from work, and with every clap of thunder, my fear intensified. It didn't matter that I was safe at home with my sister, who was deliberately attentive to me. I needed to be prepared.

Prepared for what, I don't know. It's a mystery to me what young Karen was doing on those occasions. Why was I so afraid when there was no threat of harm? I wasn't scared of the darkness of the storm, the pounding of the rain, or the claps of thunder. Was I getting ready to escape danger? My mother repeatedly warned me, "Don't let anybody in if I'm not home." She meant no harm. She was not trying to instill fear in me—she didn't want company in the house without her supervision. Yet, I believed I was unprotected. I had a compelling need to be vigilant. The storm represented something unpredictable that was out of my control. If we had to leave the house, what would I do? How would I take care of myself and be safe from bad people and things happening?

At the time, I was unsure of why I needed to be

prepared and why I had a visceral reaction to my mother's words, "Don't let anyone into the house when I'm not home." Many years later, I realized that the fear was rooted in my witnessing my oldest sister being raped when I was around 3 or 4. We were home alone at the time; she was babysitting me. The situation was so traumatic that I repressed it, yet the fear would rise within me when I heard my mother's words of caution. As an adult for many years, I had this feeling in my gut that things would happen that I would not be able to deal with effectively.

Living in fear, no matter the reason, has grave consequences. Fear paralyzes; it clouds one's vision, causing one to view the world and situations only through a lens that catastrophizes. It blocks our ability to view life with varying alternatives. Fear sees people as predators and causes one to see oneself as inadequate, unprepared, and unequipped.

Once, when I was in high school, we lived on the second floor of my Great-Aunt Neva's building. I was home from school one afternoon when the doorbell rang. I looked out the window. It was my great-uncle from Mississippi. I knew who he was, and he knew who I was.

"Karen is your mother home?" he called.

"No."

"Is Neva home?"

I said, "No."

He looked at me, and I looked at him. I let the window down and went back to what I was doing.

He rang the bell again, so I went back to the window. "Yes?" I said.

Uncle Buddy asked if he could wait in the house until my mother or Neva got home. "I drove from Mississippi," he reasoned.

I politely said, "No, my mother told me not to let anyone in when she was not home."

My uncle waited patiently for four or five hours that day until my mother came home.

Some people might interpret that as a sign of an obedient daughter; however, for me, it was a sign of an entrenched sense of fear that had no basis in reality. I knew my great-uncle possessed no ill intentions.

My uncle was forgiving. He chuckled as he shared what happened with my mother and Neva. He might not have understood why I did not let him in, but he was wise enough not to take offense.

I lived in fear for many years; well into adulthood, I was unsure if I would be able to handle unexpected situations. What if something terrible happened? Would I know what to do? Would I be left alone, vulnerable to harmful and dangerous situations and people? Who would be my advocate? Who would be my protector? It was like I expected the "boogeyman" to come to the door. I second-guessed people's motives and intent, which caused me to shrink into the background. I had to be careful to accurately discern those who entered my circle. I lived in the gloom of my fear.

Struggle shows up in our behaviors and recurring patterns. It may be in vigilance or carelessness. It reveals itself in sexual behaviors or hatred towards men, women, or other races. We see it in substance abuse and materialism. It creeps into relationships when we hang on so tight to someone they need to escape or push our loved ones away before they abandon us. Lies are voiced in aggression and anger; they hide in depression and mental illness. Lies give birth to new lies and complicate our lives. We spend time with the wrong people. We let others control us. We give away too much of ourselves. We think people owe us.

It's a shame we seek healing only when the level of pain and distress has become unbearable, but healing is possible. Wounds can heal. Pain can lessen and leave. Physical wounds require attention and proper care to avoid becoming infected. So do psychological and emotional ones. Wounds leave scars, yes, but over time, scars soften. After a time, they are barely noticeable. Some wounds need great care and recovery time while others heal quickly. We, the walking wounded, cannot blame others when they do not see our pain. Physical wounds heal first outwardly before the healing moves inward.

Do these words sound familiar to you?

I never get what I have been running after.
I just want to be free.
I want to be healed, whatever that looks like.
I can't stay here anymore; it doesn't matter what I feel later.
I no longer want to be the person I have been.

We seek healing in order to be free of what has held us back. When we do this work, our focus cannot be only on bodily healing, as critical as it is. We need to seek healing of our spirits and begin emotional healing. The same is true for emotional and psychological wounds. We must clean our wounds of the germs of guilt, shame, fear, feelings of rejection, abandonment, unworthiness, and self-doubts. Spiritual and emotional healing begins inwardly and then pours outwardly.

Are you ready to commit to a new path? If you find yourself asking questions like these, you may be ready:

Why do I keep running into these same people?
Why do I feel numb when I see others truly engaged in life?
Why do I push people away?
Why am I so afraid?

Your pain is an indication that it is time to heal. This self-awareness can bring up feelings of anguish, but it is the first step to healing.

Imagine a time not long from now when you feel peace. You are okay with who you are and where you are. You take responsibility for your own behaviors and beliefs and know you are not responsible for the behaviors and beliefs of others, especially those who harmed you.

You will breathe easily, feeling freedom from the turmoil that has kept you running in circles. You will know you faced the pain, even embraced it for a short time, in order to begin to heal. You can now live a life where there are no boundaries or restrictions. You know you can face whatever circumstances come because your feelings will not determine your future.

The first step is to be open to the journey. People return to what is familiar, even if it is uncomfortable. I ask you to be courageous. Don't let the fear of the unknown pull you back. Remember the double-minded man and his unstable ways. If we do not heal emotionally and spiritually, our emotional woundedness governs our lives. We must choose commitment to the path of healing.

The healing path will be rocky at times, and you may find yourself slipping. It can be lonely, too, because it is so personal. No one else has a path like yours. So, you must become comfortable with silence and solitude on this journey, knowing it will lead you to an abundant life with stronger relationships and clear personal boundaries. When self-doubt and negative thoughts return to us, as they will, you will want to turn back. Remember: The other path is a circle, where you return to the beginning again and again. Productive and life-giving thoughts lead us forward toward healing. I tell myself *I am worthy, I am lovable*, and you can, too. We must detach from the lies. We can detach from our guilt and shame, rejection and abandonment, and our fear of freedom.

You are not responsible for what happened to you, but you have an obligation to yourself to decide whether to perpetuate the lie you have come to believe. If it torments you, it is time to identify the lie. All of us must do this work. We must replace "it's my fault" and "I'm not good enough" with the truth. I am good enough. You are. We are.

I will be honest: This work will bring you forward to liberty, but there will be times of challenge. People often return to what is familiar, even if it is uncomfortable, painful, or distressing. This journey can be lonely, too, because it is so personal. In your pilgrimage to healing, there are places that only you can go. Just as your freedom is a place only you can embrace and thrive in.

Your work

Take some time to think about where you are in your life and consider the questions below.

1. Do you find yourself in situations where you are being mistreated or rejected or taking the blame?
2. Do you find yourself in a situation where you are mistreating others, delivering rejection, or assigning blame?
3. What is the turmoil you experience?
4. What emotions result from this turmoil?
5. When did you start feeling this way? Can you pinpoint when it started?
6. How would it feel to put this turmoil aside?

Use this space to record your thoughts.

Chapter 2

THE CHAINS THAT BIND

❧

Stand fast therefore in the liberty by which Christ has made us free, and do not be entangled again with a yoke of bondage.

—*Galatians 5:1 (NKJV)*

When our woundedness is not healed, we try to mask it. To the people around us, we are fine, we are whole, we are what they expect us to be. But again and again, we end up in situations and relationships that are not healthy, or we find ourselves acting in ways that lead us further away from the path we want to be on.

Do you find yourself asking, "Why am I faced with this problem again?" or "Why do I always attract these types of people?" or "Why do I keep responding in this way when I know it doesn't work?"

We are bound by chains made of lies. They bind us tightly with the beliefs we have built from our past experiences—sometimes passed down to us from generations before—and alter our perceptions and mentalities. With the chains wrapped around us, it becomes difficult to feel worthy of love, to feel capable, to feel good enough. Like the unbearably uncomfortable hair shirts worn by people in early Christian religious orders to remind themselves to remain penitent, we wear our chains. We have come to believe we are meant to carry them like Steven, who harbors a belief that he is an imposter, whose financial security does not bring him comfort even though it was earned through his hard work. His experiences with childhood poverty led him to believe there is not enough to go around, and he must remain uncomfortable and vigilant around money, even when comfort and business growth are easily within reach. His chains, these lies, are heavy.

There are endless variations of Steven's story because the chains of one person are not the same as those of another. Take Sandra, for instance, who also experienced poverty as a child. Her experience contributed to her belief that she is perpetually in a state of lack, even when reality says differently. Sandra went to school and followed the path of success to wealth. But living in poverty as a child was so traumatic for her that it is now what she fears most, and that fear keeps her bound to an unsustainable lifestyle. *I don't have enough*, she tells herself. She protects herself by building a fortress of high-end household goods and regularly treats herself to name-brand clothing and spa treatments. She shops to ward off her fear of going without. Her lifestyle leaves her without savings, but with each purchase, she convinces herself she has a place in the world. Like Job in the Old Testament, what she greatly feared is now upon her.

Can you feel the weight of your chains? Chains hold us in place and stop us from moving forward. With them, we can ignore the woundedness of our being.

Use this space to record your thoughts.

Marcus, one of my patients, used to hate the deep brown complexion of his skin. He hated to look at himself in the mirror. The darkness of his skin made him feel dirty. The taunts of children at school told him he was. Marcus believed he was dirty for most of his life. He comes from a large family of twenty-two children. With twenty-two kids and only one parent earning money, times were tough for everyone in his family. There was not much to go around. What the other children at school told him may have been true at the time. It is entirely likely Marcus was dirty as a child—clean clothes being reliant on water service—but he isn't anymore. He is an adult now, a remarkable man in my view, and he takes great care in his ablutions. He showers daily and launders his clothes regularly. The trouble is that his chains are strong. He believes the lie despite the facts. He looks in the mirror and sees the shame he felt as a child, and it looks like the darkness of his skin.

Lifting our chains takes enormous effort. We internalize what people have said to us, often years before, and these beliefs operate under our consciousness even though they are not the truth. I am certain you can think of times from your childhood when someone made a comment that left you in a perpetual state of doubt for years. It left you in fear, and you likely kept it a secret, which allowed it to grow from doubt into belief.

The Book of Job asks essential questions about the human condition and the meaning of suffering. In it, Job is a wealthy man and a rich landowner who raises livestock. God himself describes Job as "blameless and upright," someone who turns away from sin and temptation. Yet, in a series of unfortunate events, Job loses everything: wealth, livelihood, and ten children. He becomes ill, his body covered in sores, and lives in agonizing pain.

His friends and family tell him to turn away from God and encourage him to blame God for his troubles, but he does not. They suggest Job did something wrong to deserve his suffering, implying he is not as upright as they thought him to be. Job comes close to believing it. He sinks into his anguish and wonders why he should continue to live and to hope. He feels his suffering is unjust. He listens to his friends for far too long as they try to convince him he is not a decent man favored by God. For a time, Job begins to participate in the lies, and even though his faith remains strong, he allows doubt to surface. He nearly agrees to accept the chains and carry their weight.

Our suffering is not fair. You did not ask to exist in woundedness, nor did Job do anything to cause his suffering. Neither did Marcus. Suffering has nothing to do with our conduct, values, or morals (although that is not to say that there are no consequences to one's choices or behaviors). What is remarkable about Job and Marcus is how they stood fast in their commitment to hope, even in the face of crushing pain and doubt. Neither man turned away from the effort of removing the chains that bind.

Despite Marcus's pain and past trauma, something inside of him tugged at his spirit, telling him, *Your past does not dictate who you are and it certainly does not dictate your future.* He began to challenge his thoughts. It was not his deep brown complexion that made him "dirty," but the very real circumstances of living in poverty—the absence of running water to bathe and detergent to wash his clothes. With the lies uncovered, Marcus began to see his life more clearly. He was not his childhood circumstances; his clothes may have been dirty and sometimes he could not bathe, but he was not dirty, and his deep brown skin was definitely not dirty. He began to realize that he was no longer that little boy and no longer living in those circumstances.

Although Marcus' struggle was not over with this realization, he began to see himself through a lens through which he was self-sufficient. His pain gave over to possibility and purpose. He explored the possibility that he could be a protector and advocate for children living in great poverty, mental illness, and self-hatred, as he had. He determined he would be the first in his family to attend college. He sought out resources that would help him get there. He fought his fear, and, at times, negative beliefs came forward, especially when his family and others intentionally or unintentionally perpetuated the lies from his past. They even discouraged him from furthering his education and seeking a life outside of what he knew as a child. Marcus refused to see himself through the dark lenses of his past. Instead, he viewed himself through corrective lenses of hope and healing. He held tightly to the vision of going to college to get his bachelor's degree. As his vision became clearer, he saw himself getting a master's degree and working as a social worker.

Marcus' struggle led him to work with people who experienced struggles similar to his own. I have seen in Marcus an incredible determination to remain free, detached from his traumatic past and the pain of the chains that kept him bound. I am reminded of a film I saw recently, where the main character, an artist, struggles to heal and forgive. Finally, having moved past his childhood trauma, he finds himself free. Using a box-cutter, with precision, he carefully cuts out his own image from the piece of art that represents his past pain. This scene represents how he moved beyond his past pain by forgiving himself, his father, and even his mother for loving his father. It is through their commitment to forgiveness and self-love that both Marcus and this character could see and embrace the purpose in their pain.

As for Job, he did not turn away from God. He resisted the doubts placed upon him by his family and friends, and he hung on to the remnants of his faith. He told himself; *I am worthy of the love of God. I will continue to praise God despite my circumstances.* This commitment saved him in the end, and God restored everything to Job that he had lost, not as a reward, but as an acknowledgment Job had engaged in the difficult work of questioning the lies.

Woundedness can be healed, but the journey is near impossible when you carry your chains. Moving forward with their weight slows you down. Exhaustion will raise your fears and doubts, and you can be convinced to turn back—to old behaviors and habits and to the people who gain from the lies you learned to believe. Job and Marcus recognized they were becoming bound up in erroneous beliefs; they knew the suffering would continue unless they acknowledged their woundedness and their deep fears. Each man had to seek out the lies parading as the truth. They had to stop agreeing to it because they knew how much credence and power they gave to the lies when they continued to participate in them. By turning away from untruths, misinterpretations, and myths, they reclaimed personal power. By acknowledging their own responsibility in perpetuating the lies, they could deny the power in what was falsely given. When we refuse to lift off the chains of misbelief, we agree to participate in the lies. Marcus told himself, "Yes, I am dirty." Even Job, for a moment, agreed with his friends, thinking, "Yes, I do deserve my suffering." They were wounded and then wrapped in chains.

I do not mean to imply that you accept blame. Yes, people have hurt you, they have wounded you, and they have to be accountable for their role. Yes, you do need to place the onus on them for what they did that caused you to feel inadequate or fearful. They must be responsible for their behavior, but they are not responsible for how you carried it.

My mother bore the weight of many chains, some I will never know or understand. At the end of her life, as she was transitioning out of this world, I heard her reckoning with the questions she had not yet resolved. "You can't have my children!" she would cry out. "Why didn't my mother love me?" she asked.

Decades before, when I was a child, my mother went into the hospital for surgery. We were sent to live with relatives. That experience brought up a lot of fear in her. She had made a promise to herself that she would never give away any of her children, like her mother had been forced to. She never wanted her children to feel the way she had, like she was not wanted, like something was wrong with her to cause her mother to give her away. The fact that she was given up at birth and sent to live with her great-aunt, which was not unusual in my culture, wounded her. My mother struggled with the belief that she must have done something wrong: Her mother could not have loved her if she gave her away but kept her younger siblings, who were born several years after her. She battled these self-beliefs all her life, a fact I saw in those last days. The real battle was that, in her adult mind, she understood the circumstances that resulted in her living with Aunt Babe, but the little girl inside could not reconcile with the rationale offered by her adult self.

My mother did well. She raised good children. She kept her promise and raised all of us on her own. There was a time when a man, a good man, wanted to marry her, but she turned him down. She always said, "I don't want anybody to be over my children." I think my mother turned him down because of her chains; she needed to prove that she was able to take care of her children and show all the nay-sayers that they were wrong, and she did just that. My mother passed away four years ago, but that fear, and negative words spoken over her kept her in bondage, in chains. That self-promise, *I'll never give my children away*, was a good promise, but it was based on an oppressive belief. She was wounded deeply and bound by the chains of belief.

It can be shameful at first when we recognize how we participated in the abuse or harm—how willingly we carried the weight of our chains. We need to forgive ourselves for our participation, but first, we need to untangle our beliefs and separate the truth from the lies. When the lies are lifted from our bodies, we can make room for productive and life-giving thoughts that will lead us toward healing. You will be able to tell yourself you are worthy of love, and you are loving.

Your work

1. Are you carrying chains that bind you to untruths or beliefs that no longer serve you? Explore your chains and how you carry them with these questions below.
2. Whose voice are you hearing when you face a choice? Is it truly yours?
3. Who has been in control of your beliefs?
4. Which of your thoughts needs to be reconsidered?
5. What are you getting out of staying stuck?
6. What are you afraid of?
7. What would it feel like to be your own advocate?

Use this space to record your thoughts.

Chapter 3
WHO TOLD YOU THAT?

You shall refute every tongue that rises against you in judgment.

—Isaiah 54:17 (ESV)

There is greatness in all of us. You may not see it today, but it is there, waiting to manifest in you. Greatness is not based on our senses. It is not what we see, hear, touch, or experience. Greatness is beyond or above that. When you finally become aware of it, you realize there is a place for you.

The voices we carry within us can overpower us, so much so that we begin to believe them because we cannot hear anything else. When the voices are based on lies, they become harmful.

You're dumb.
You'll never be anything.
You're just like your mother.
You're exactly like your father.
You're ugly. Nobody would find you attractive.
Nobody likes you. They're just pretending to like you.
The only thing you're good for is sex.
You can't be trusted with that responsibility. You'll only mess it up.

I want to ask you: Who told you that?

The tongue has power. Sometimes, people say things to you in judgment. They hurt you deeply. They criticize you, run you down, or take away your power. They do it deliberately or with simple callousness and ignorance, unaware you are listening.

Language is powerful. Each time we speak, we plant a seed. I attended a sermon recently where the pastor offered this analogy: "With seeds, they sprout, they bud, they bloom, and they produce." Who sowed the seed that became rooted in your soul? Was it your mother, father, teacher, or someone from down the block? You only needed to hear it once, didn't you, before it began to sprout? Who told you that?

Voices from our past eventually become our own.

The words we remember are hurtful and shameful, so we keep them to ourselves. We water and protect them until they sprout into our hearts and spirit. Eventually, their roots grow deep; we no longer remember when they were not there. We might not recall who said it, but we accept what the voices said. The plant sprouts and buds, and it blooms inside of us. Eventually, it produces fruit that shows up in our behaviors and worldviews. We no longer need to hear those people speak those words again because we have begun repeating them to ourselves. We let the voices guide our actions. We shrink back from opportunities. We make self-defeating choices.

Lynelle has more than a great singing voice or talent passed down generationally. Her voice is angelic, and she might become one of the biggest names in music. When she sings, she touches my soul; I can feel the presence of God. It is as though God himself is ministering to me.

Lynnette never pursued music outside of her church. At a young age, her talent was already recognized in the church and community. People told her she was meant for musical greatness. At home, though, her mother's words pierced deeply. With good intentions, meaning to keep Lynelle grounded, her mother would tell her "Don't get a big head" and "Don't get all puffed up."

The word *integrity* has Latin roots in *integer*, which means complete and whole, undivided, possessing an inner unity and coherence. As humans, we seek wholeness. With integrity, we cannot rest easy in situations of uncertainty or complexity because we have a code to follow. So, when we are told lies or when we translate actions and words into meaning, we internalize our new knowledge, right or wrong, seeking to become whole. Lynnette took her mother's words to heart. She interpreted her mother's words to mean *my mother finds my voice aggravating*. What she knew to be true about herself was no longer in integrity with her mother's view; there was division. To become whole again, she would have to choose what to believe. In Lynnette's case, Integrity is based on knowing that you were given an innate gift and using it to bless and edify others, while having a "big head" means being puffed up and conceited.

That day, Lynette was chained by her mother's words. She pursued music outside the church and would often sing for church events when asked, but she no longer shared her gifts through the ministry of healing and worship as she once loved.

Early in life, when we look to others for guidance on navigate navigating the world, we accept their words and actions as truth. We build our inner worlds by interpreting the world around us. When harsh words tell us to remain small, we live small. We quickly translate a look or an action into our belief because we learn how to interpret tone and body language early in life. Like Lynette, she interprets her mother's words as saying she should not pursue her dreams and allow her gift to manifest in its fullness just based on her mother's words. Indeed, it was not her mother's intent to stifle her gift of song and worship, but those few words altered Lynette's perception of who she was and who she should be.

Don Miguel Ruiz, author of *The Four Agreements*, told a similar story about a young girl who lost her voice. He describes how we build our worldview through the concept of agreement. "There are thousands of agreements you have made with yourself," he writes, "with other people, with your dream of life, with God, with society, with your parents, with your spouse, with your children. But the most important agreements are the ones you made with yourself.... In these agreements, you say, 'This is what I am. This is what I believe. I can do certain things and some things I cannot do. This is reality, that is fantasy; this is possible, that is impossible.'"[1] We permit the words of others to enter our hearts and

1. Ruiz, D. M. (1997). *The four agreements illustrated edition: A practical guide to personal freedom.* Amber-Allen Publishing.

minds because it is too difficult to hold opposing ideas of ourselves. We seek integrity.

Lynette's mother likely didn't realize she was planting a seed that would yield a poisonous fruit. However, Lynette took those words to heart and believed she did not deserve confidence and recognition. Her gift was stunted, and she could no longer minister to and heal her community with her music.

To find freedom from lies, you must first identify the voice of the lies you agree to believe. Then, you must find the voices of truth overwhelmed by shame, guilt, embarrassment, or anger. They are quieter, older, and unsure. They sound like this:

I am myself, unique and worthy.
I have a lot to give to a romantic partner.
I can be responsible and trustworthy.
I can relinquish the harms of the past.
I have the right to every gift the universe can offer.
I have the power to change my circumstances.
I have everything I need to figure out what to do.
I am beautiful as I am.
I have greatness within me.

The Bible story of the Twelve Spies reminds us that we cannot always trust the voices of others. In it, God tells Moses that he is bestowing the land of Canaan to the Israelites. They can walk through the doors of the city and call it their own, God tells them, but he advises Moses to send a dozen men to explore it first. Moses listens and sends the men on a reconnaissance mission. He asks the men to return with a report on whether the soil is fertile and decadent and whether the inhabitants are strong or weak.

The men leave on their mission. When they reach Canaan, they discover fertile land. They taste sweet grapes, pomegranates, and figs. The cities there are significant and fortified, and the people show great strength. It is indeed the land God described to Moses: Canaan flows with milk and honey.

When the men return, they present themselves to Moses and the community, but their optimism has diminished. Fear has set in among ten of them. They agree that God has offered a bountiful gift, but they are doubtful that the Israelites could claim the land. The inhabitants are too strong to be defeated, they report, and their fear causes them to turn to deceit and fabrication. The size and strength of the Canaanites is too great.

"They are giants!" the ten men say. "They are so big,

like giants, and we are only the size of grasshoppers in their midst. There is no way we can wrestle Canaan from such fearsome monsters!"

The news devastates the community, and despair takes over. They believe the lies of the ten men.

The remaining two men, Joshua and Caleb, speak up then, and they insist on the truth. "There were no giants," they insist. "If the Lord is so pleased with us to offer us such respite, they argue, then we can defeat the inhabitants, strong as they are, and claim Canaan as our own. We must have faith in God's promise."

But the community already believes the lies so fervently that the Israelites nearly stone Caleb and Jacob in anger.

The ten spies had spoken out of fear. They had expressed their sense of smallness and futility in the face of a big challenge. The community heard their words and took them to heart; the lies became so deeply rooted that no one could hear the truth when it was spoken.

Who were the ten spies in your life? Who told you that you are not good enough? Who makes you feel guilt, embarrassment, or shame? More importantly, who were the Joshuas and Calebs in your life who tried to dispel the lies? Who will give you a good report and let you break free of your chains so you can fulfill your promise?

As with Lynette and the twelve spies, we must

determine what report we will believe, whether it is ours or someone else's. Will we choose to acknowledge the challenges of life and ignore the infinite possibilities of life? Lynette had a God-given angelic voice, not just a singing talent. She was faced with believing that her voice was a gift from God to be shared in its fullness or drawback because of the planted fear of having a big head.

Use this space to record your thoughts.

_____

_____

_____

_____

_____

_____

_____

_____

_____

_____

I asked you earlier, "Who told you that?" As I mentioned, sometimes the words were spoken so long ago that you might not even know who told you, but you struggle with your internalized beliefs. Your struggle may seem normal. *Don't all people have these challenges?* you think.

Sometimes, someone else comes along and sees your struggle before you do. It happened to me when I was in my late twenties. It was my first job, and I had only been working for six to eight months. At that time, I was married, and my daughter was two. I was trying to figure out who I was. All the uncertainties and pain of my past were tormenting me, and I didn't even know it. I knew the longing to be the someone who was trapped inside me. I knew there was something more to me, but my internal struggles blinded me. I believed I was not lovable and worthy of acceptance. Others around me would have been surprised to know this about me. How could I feel such confusion? I was attractive and well-groomed, married, with a supportive husband and a baby. I wore the mask well.

One day, Mohammed, an older colleague, pulled me aside. "Once you realize who you are," he said, "and once you see yourself as I do, you will understand your greatness."

I did not fully understand what he was telling me. What did he mean? When I asked him about it, he said, "You'll figure it out."

As my life unfolded, I began to see what he was talking about. He must have seen my struggle, maybe in my interactions with people or how I carried myself. He saw not only the devastation of the lies I believed in but also the greatness within me. He could see both my present and my future. What he was really saying was, "Where you are now is not where you are going to end up."

Two voices beat within your breast. Tara Leigh Cobble spoke truth when she wrote that line in her poem.[2] All of us carry within us lies we interpret as truth. They are strong and bear poor fruit. In your life, you will find yourself repeating behavior and thought patterns. Here is what you need to know: They hold you back. You must listen to the voices of life that promise greatness and freedom. If they have been silent for too long, it may be difficult to hear them, so seek out the people who believe in you. Turn towards the people who will speak louder than the lies. Listen to them. Listen to the Mohammeds.

What is most important to remember is that the truth is strong, but you must water it and let it take root. Give

2. Tara Leigh Cobble. (n.d.). AZQuotes.com. Retrieved January 08, 2025, from AZQuotes.com Web site: https://www.azquotes.com/quote/1497636

it sun, and it will sprout. As you do in your garden, thin out the seedlings, pull out the lies, and make room in the soil for the seedlings that produce life. I didn't hear Mohammed's message of greatness right away. We must tend to our seedlings of truth while they root; eventually, they will bloom and bear fruit. You will hear them tell you the truth: *You are good, deserving, and worthy of an abundant life*. Seeing my life unfold before my eyes, I began to follow my dreams and put fear and concern about how others saw me behind me. I was able to know that I had something special in me, as we all do, and I was able to embrace Mohammed's words. They were like a full tank of gas poured into a stalled car left on the side of the road. His words propelled me forward toward freedom from my past. There will be people you encounter who will also speak words of life as you travel the journey of life. We all have Mohammeds assigned to us.

Luke 8:15 speaks of sowing seeds (the promises of God) on good ground and yielding succulent fruit in harvest time: "But the ones that fell on the good ground are those who, having heard the word with a noble and good heart, keep it and bear fruit with patience" (NKJV). Whose report will you believe? What will you grow?

Your work

1. What recurring voices or beliefs have you internalized?
2. Who told you that? Who was speaking?
3. What role did you take in cultivating those voices?
4. At what point did they stop speaking and you became the speaker?
5. Do the voices speak life or lies?
6. What harvest have you reaped? What torment came to you as a result of words you heard spoken?
7. Has it come in the form of addiction, self-hatred, perpetual failures, procrastination, self-sabotage, and fear of success?
8. Who in your life has seen your greatness? Who spoke of life to you, like Mohammed?

Use this space to record your thoughts.

Chapter 4
DON'T BELIEVE THE LIES

Death and life are in the power of the tongue, and those who love it will eat its fruits.

—Proverbs 18:21 (ESV)

It is Friday night, and Daria is out for a celebratory dinner with her husband. Tonight, they are splurging a little, recognizing her hard-earned promotion. Thanks to the raise and the extra paid time off, life will be a little easier now. They can have money for a down payment on a home and to take a vacation this summer. The future is promising, and they enjoy their dinner.

In the taxi home, Daria is quiet. She feels uneasy. Her success feels precarious. Yes, sure, she is getting a raise, but what about the new tax bracket? Will it eat up all her new earnings?

Over the weekend, subtle self-sabotage creeps in. Is she genuinely qualified for the job? The interview went well, but she worries she can't live up to the new responsibilities. Daria tries self-talk. *I earned this promotion. I worked hard for it. It was a fair interview process. I am the best person for this job.* Her words are hard to hear over her anxiety and doubt. By Monday, she is dressing for work with apprehension. Her confidence has dropped, and she is nearly late for her first day because she let her doubts have power.

It sounds familiar, doesn't it? When faced with change and opportunity, we feel an urge to step back. Where we should feel joy in progress, we instead feel a nagging uncertainty, a hesitation to fully embrace the new path. For those of us who are bound by chains of old lies, it is even more difficult to walk forward; the weight pulls us down, pulls us back. Have you felt torn between the person you are and the person you aspire to become? Turning back to what you know seems easier in those moments.

Now, as you confront lies that have tethered you to a life that no longer serves you, you stand at the start of a new path that will lead you to profound change. It is a pivotal moment where you acknowledge the gravity of past beliefs and still, despite your fear, walk toward the future. I want you to listen to the sound of life and step toward it. I want you to leave behind the chaos and the confusion. You have a right to greatness.

It is not unrealistic to want to be better than we are. We have greatness within us already. If we want to grow, we must leave behind the lies and the pain. Our hearts and minds will believe us when we change the message, but we must continue to tell ourselves that we are enough and deserve to know our greatness.

Tell yourself this: *I can manage right now, so I can manage with what comes next. I'd rather manage this challenge than continue living with the pain I carry.*

Some of us have tried to change our circumstances more than once. Two steps forward, it seems, then three steps back. We choose to turn away from the life that is holding us back and go forth, but then we step back. We look at the path in front of us and fear the journey ahead. It seems we must face a battle in front of us and another one behind us. We have no good choice, except to see ourselves as we want to be.

That's the battle Melyssa is facing now. Melyssa came to me for therapy because she could not leave her relationship with her boyfriend. He is mistreating her, and although she knows she must leave him and although she is financially secure and has taken steps to leave, even finding a new place to live, she cannot find it in herself to break up with him. On the surface, it didn't make a lot of sense, neither to her friends nor to her, but when we dug deeper into her fears, she began to understand it more clearly. She's afraid of being abandoned. She is more afraid of feeling abandoned than she is afraid of her boyfriend's mistreatment. Now, Melyssa needs to face her fear. If she doesn't, her life will remain the same. She will continue to struggle.

People who have moved through addiction recovery will understand this battle. Freedom comes when you face the pain, but before you come to that realization, you believe freedom comes from the alcohol, or the food, or the sex, or the shopping, or codependency. It's disheartening to be back where we started, to know that we must try again to lift off the chains that bind us to a life of pain. It is devastating. We believe the lies we were told. We say:

I'm not made for that life.
She didn't really love me. No one could.
I can't quit. It's too hard. The addiction is too powerful.
I don't deserve that responsibility.

If you are surrounded by people who are uncomfortable in the life you have left behind, they will confirm your doubts. They may not say it aloud, but you imagine their thoughts all the same. "Who are you to achieve greatness?" they say. "Why should you be the one to do that? You're not that smart, not that good, not that capable." The prospect of change terrifies those ensconced in their comfort zones. You are terrified, too. It would be easier to stay back in the place where you know the rules, you know what to expect, and you know how to behave. You want to be successful and finally free of pain, but you wonder:

Now that I am free, what will be required of me?
What will this new life look like?
Do I really belong there?

This is the power of the lies. Over time, we internalize them, and they guide our behavior and choices. They take us by the hand and lead us to a place of pain. But that is when you must take up the battle. That is the moment to visualize and speak of the future you want. What if you can turn away from the lies and believe the truth? What will your life look like?

Use this space to record your thoughts.

_____

_____

_____

_____

_____

_____

The people who want us to give up and stay back are dream snatchers. Beware of dream snatchers. Recognize that they, too, are weighed down by chains. They have also attached themselves to lies they heard long ago. You will recognize a dream snatcher when you encounter one. A dream snatcher tries to distract you or cause you to abandon your dreams by introducing negative thoughts and ideas into your psyche. Their sole purpose is to get you to abort your dreams so that they will never come to fruition.

A dream snatcher may tell you that people like you can never accomplish such a task. Your thinking is too grandiose, you are not smart enough, or you just don't have what it takes.

Voices have power. As the Book of Proverbs says, they can speak of life, or they can speak of death. Which one will you need to listen to now if you want to leave the pain behind? Which one will undermine your greatness with words of defeat? Contemplate the weight of your own words, too, recognizing the potential for chaos or clarity that lies within every syllable.

It is your time to speak. Life and death are in the power of the tongue. You can't speak life and then speak death and expect to go anywhere. That creates a life of chaos and confusion for yourself. If something is bringing you life and lighting you up, focus on that, and leave the pain behind.

Self-belief is the cornerstone of meaningful change. But when changes come, we become scared, and we self-sabotage. Like Daria when she got her promotion, we repeat the untruths we have internalized. But what if you are the person you desire to be already? Daria is. Her bosses know it. Her colleagues know it. Her spouse knows it. She needs to believe it. Daria must challenge the inner voices telling her she doesn't deserve her promotion. This is the moment where she must speak louder and tell herself, *Take a chance on your capabilities. Listen to the people who believe in your greatness. Don't be your own dream snatcher.*

I had a vivid dream once that I have remembered for years. In it, my cousin Carlotta and I were still children. We were holding hands and running towards what appeared to be an old, abandoned high-rise. The grayish bricks were dirty and worn down, and the loosened mortar fell from between them. We entered the building together. The only lighting came from the sunrise shining through the many windows. We soon found ourselves standing in front of the elevator. When the doors swooshed open, I got in. I wanted to explore the floors above. But Carlotta dropped my hand and wouldn't step foot into the elevator.

"Are you coming?" I asked.

"No, I can't," she said. She knew she couldn't go with me. I watched her as the elevator doors closed.

The elevated dipped and rose, leaving Carlotta on the floor below me.

The dream may have been inspired by true events. That year, my sister and I found ourselves being bussed each day from our neighborhood to a Catholic school in an all-White community. My mother, having been told that she was nothing and her children would never become anyone worthwhile, stressed the importance of a good education and instilled the belief that we could accomplish anything if we worked hard. She wanted us to have the best education, which in her mind would afford us the opportunity to succeed in life. So, that year, we had to be brave and navigate a new community.

During my first year at this all-White school, my mother was told that I needed to repeat the fourth grade. No one ever explained to me why, and I don't recall my mother ever questioning it, but I knew it was not right. I did not struggle academically. That could not be the reason for holding me back. I decided, then, I had to prove myself. I knew I must choose to listen to the voices of life. I didn't say *I am a failure; I am dumb, I was held back*. If you already know the end of the story, why would you move forward? I had to move forward. I had to tell myself, *You're smart, you can do anything.* Those voices of life fueled me and pushed me to go beyond what anyone else around me was able to do. I don't know of any classmates who attained my level of education. I was young, and I hadn't learned to turn away from all the lies underlying my beliefs in most ways yet, but I had the skills to do it in this area of my life. My interpretation of my dream with Carlotta was that I stepped onto the elevator because I wanted to rise, knowing that I might have to leave behind a familiar life.

Listen to this story of small thinking. Once, there was a genie who gave a man one wish. The man thought and thought about what he truly wanted.

"What I truly want," he said, "is a golf club."

The genie nodded, and suddenly, an upscale country club appeared before him. The building was beautiful, with golf carts parked in front. Inside was a gourmet restaurant where the stars of the golf world gathered to reminisce about their wins. It was incredible, better than the man had imagined.

"But I only wanted a golf club," he said, "a new driver. Not a—a—golf club!"

The genie slapped his knee and let out a belly laugh. "Silly man! I knew that. But you didn't dream big enough. Now you can golf with the greats."

Ephesians 3:20 says, "Now unto him that is able to do exceeding abundantly above all that we ask or think, according to the power that worketh in us…" (ESV). Many of us dream small. We can't believe that we can have more, and if we dream big, there is no way our dreams will ever manifest. Internally, we can see big dreams happening for others around us and even people we do not directly know, but not for us because we believe in limiting lies. You must believe that you can have more than a little bit. You are worthy of it. Just like you've attached yourself to the lies, you can attach yourself to what you want. You might aim to make six figures, imagining a good life when you make over a hundred thousand dollars. But six figures can be two hundred thousand or nine hundred thousand. What if you aim for a million? A billion? If you believe six figures is possible, why not seven? You believed the voices that spoke lies, after all. If you choose to believe the lies, you can choose to believe in your dreams. Choosing to give attention to the voice that speaks life into your dreams will ignite a paradigm shift in your thinking: thoughts will change, and so will your behavior. Attach yourself to what is life-giving. Banish the lies you meditated on; meditate on your hope.

I am brilliant.
I am creative.
I am capable.

I am deserving of greatness.
I am uniquely made in the image of my father,
my creator.
I am who God says I am.

If you want to be free, you must see yourself as free. If you want to have friends, you can't sit back and be mean to others; you must be friendly. Write a vision of what you want. Imagine yourself free. Write the vision, make it plain: *I will not attach myself to anything associated with death, only things that are life-giving.* That's how you stop the chatter. Put it on paper, write the details, and meditate on it. Write the integral details of your dreams and how you want to see yourself. It must be more than positive thinking and affirmations. What you say and see must connect with your inner spirit. You must see and feel it as though it is happening in real-time.

Your work

1. What is your deepest desire? Capture it with as many details as possible.
2. Who are the dream snatchers around you? Identify the lies they tell and counteract them with the opposite truth.
3. What if you did succeed?
4. What does your greatness look like?
5. If you had a genie, what would you wish for? Consider what the genie might wish for you.

Use this space to record your thoughts.

Chapter 5

YOU ARE NOT
WHAT HAPPENED TO YOU

❦

*In all these things we are more than conquerors
through him who loved us.*

—Romans 8:37 (NIV)

Imagine a future where your woundedness is no longer holding you back, a place of peace, where the trials of living have eased, and you can enjoy your greatness. We all dream of a place in our future where we are secure, a place where we can rest easy and know our purpose and the purpose of our pain.

You can have it. If you have been living in a place of woundedness, you already have what you need to face the challenges still in front of you. You have persistence and resilience on your side. I like to remind myself of Matthew 19:26: "With God, all things are possible" (ESV). You need to make a choice now between which of your skills and strengths you need most now and which ones you should leave behind. It is more about thoughts and belief systems than skills. Some beliefs are not conducive to advancement and growth. These belief systems must be left behind to live out your greatness and free yourself from past chains that bind you. In your character, you already have what it takes to reach a place of greatness. You are a conqueror because you have learned to persevere.

If you are here, you have acknowledged your woundedness. You are unhappy with how it is showing up in your life, how you find yourself tied to lies and misbeliefs. You are beginning to understand how you took on these lies become your own and how that decision led you in circles. You know you cannot keep returning to the same place.

Here is where you will pivot and step onto a new path into your future. There are battles ahead, yes, tribulations to overcome, but you have what you need to push forward. Your potential and purpose are there, waiting to greet you on the other side if you embrace bravery. Will you step forward?

Right now, you may feel surprised to find yourself experiencing a sense of loss. When we realize we are living under lies and living a life bound by chains, we may experience difficult emotions. There is a sense of sadness and grief that comes along with the understanding that we lost time thanks to our woundedness. It can seem, in reflection, that we lost opportunities to explore our potential or lost the ability to live a life that is meaningful. Indeed, we may have lost love or connection with people who are important to us. We begin to count our losses, big and small, and they add up. If, in your exploration of your pain, you find yourself emotional, sad, or teary, this is normal and to be expected. Pay attention to where the grief lies because it is pointing you toward your values, which may have been buried underneath the layers of lies you told yourself in order to survive and make sense of the world.

Recently, I was speaking to Jason, a former military man who was struggling to understand his place in life. According to him, he was the black sheep of his family, the middle child who felt like he could not live up to the achievements of his siblings. Jason described feeling like an outsider, a loser. And then his experience in the Army had convinced him this was true. Rather than placing him in a job he was confident in as a cook, the Army told

Jason he was to be a mechanic. He did his best, but he couldn't grasp it. The hands-on mechanical work was a struggle. Over time, Jason sank into a severe depression and found himself drinking and becoming involved in unlawful activities. He had convinced himself the lies were true: he would never be good at anything; he was a loser. His behavior convinced others as well.

This was years ago. Today, Jason has a master's degree in education, and he has dedicated many years to teaching and advocating for children with special needs. After retiring from the role of educator, he began working as a cook at a local elementary school, a role much like the one he wanted years ago. Jason's destiny was not only to feed the body but also the souls of those who many see as not good enough, the outcasts of the world. There was purpose in his pain.

I said to him, "Let me review. Between getting out of the Army and attending school, you got a bachelor's and a master's degree in special education. You taught for many years. And then you became an advocate for children with special needs to ensure they got the services they needed."

He nodded.

"Well, you know," I said, "you sound like a shining star. Not a black sheep."

Jason looked at me. "Well, I never thought about it like this before."

I continued. "If you think about it, you were created

to be a helper, a servant. The Army was trying to put you in a box that was not in alignment with your purpose in life. When you couldn't adjust to such a life, the system, in a sense, discarded you because you were not fulfilling your purpose. You know," I said, "even if I don't compare you to anybody else, you are a shining star."

Jason had been mourning a life he felt he could have had if only he hadn't felt so disconnected. What he didn't see until that moment was how he had internalized the lies and his misbeliefs. His vision of himself had been clouded by the lies.

When we come to such discoveries about ourselves, we unearth the seeds of purpose. The breakthrough is in the awakening to the possibility that we're not the black sheep or someone who deserves scraps; we are not the problem, and our self-hatred is not justified. *Maybe*, we begin to wonder, *I'm the opposite of what I thought all these years*. With that thought also comes another: *All these years I've stayed stuck in a place I didn't belong*. Jason's story shows us how we nurture these lies long after they have our actual attention.

Even when we know better, when we reason it out and apply logic, it is difficult to set aside what we have accepted for so long. Our emotions and beliefs bind us tightly, and sometimes we need to spend time unraveling ourselves from them. A friend of mine, Russell, was sorting through photos of his father in the wake of his dad's death. He had all sorts of photos of his father's life.

But even though Russell believed he was loved as a child, his father had been unavailable often, and when he was there, he was harsh and judgmental of his son. Russell grew to feel ambivalence towards his father, and now, sorting through the photos, he had to face the fact that he had been wounded by his father and, as a result, did not feel the emotions he thought he should have for his dad. Now, after his dad's death, the pictures were framed and ready to hang, but Russell could not bring himself to put the pictures on the wall. Russell had to acknowledge that all his feelings could be true. He could love his father and also feel hurt. His father wounded him with words and left him feeling abandoned by his absence.

It is when we are facing these memories and emotions that we must remember this: we are not what happened to us. Our purpose and potential are not defined by what was done to us or spoken to us or even by what we came to believe. When we confront our difficult emotions, it is like we are facing a bully who tells us terrible things. We know the bully's words are not true, but we wonder, *What if they are? What if?*

We know that bullies are bigger in our minds than they are in reality. We know, don't we, that if we face a bully, they usually run away and retreat. The only way to rid yourself of a bully is to stand up for yourself and refuse to accept their harm. Most bullies are very fragile; they are the walking wounded, and to hide their own woundedness, they lash out at other people to cause hurt.

Your thoughts are doing the same to you, and you must stand up to them.

Reflection takes practice. It asks you to be courageous. If you have been working through the reflective questions at the end of each chapter, you may wonder if doing this work is worth it. For some of us, this reflective practice has undoubtedly intensified our pain. It isn't easy to think back on our deep hurts and examine our wounds. It is especially hard when we realize we hold some responsibility, how we allowed our wounds to gape open all this time without a barrier of protection and how our best efforts to heal fell short.

But trauma and lies live long in silence. When we face the ugliness of these wounds, we can break the chains that hold us to a life of chaos and pain, one that we do not belong to or have remain. If you haven't yet, turn back to the prompts for reflection in the earlier chapters. Spend time meditating on them. Do the work of un-silencing. This can take the form of journaling, in writing or as recorded audio diaries, or it can be done through movement and voice. Bring your thoughts outside of your body. Organize your thoughts in creative action.

Some readers will feel relief and catharsis in this reflective work. Some of you will find it painful, emotionally or physically. I want you to monitor your body's reactions.

Expect discomfort and stop your work if you feel unsafe. It is okay to pause where you are in your growth, set aside the work to heal, or seek out therapy or other professional support. This work is a process, and the results you want do not come sooner by rushing through it too quickly. Gird your strength before you return to this work. Taking a break can be a part of self-care. It doesn't mean failure. It just means that you've grown to the extent that you can right now. Say to yourself, "I choose me and self-care."

If you take a pause, make sure you commit to resuming the journey when you're ready.

If you are saying, "Yeah, this is difficult. But I'm ready to do the work," let's move forward to the future you imagine.

As the years pass, we tend to mold the past into a shape that makes sense. We need to challenge ourselves now to look at the past outside of our current understanding of it. If we have been living and making decisions based on lies, the past may not be what we thought it was. We need to go back and build a new timeline. As you do your reflective work, try to separate your past experiences from your identity. The places where you feel pain are signposts, pointing you to what you believe is important and what you stand for as a human being. These are your values.

For some of us, it is difficult to remember when our lives changed, and our self-belief shifted. Writing a timeline will help you understand, and you can do it in various ways. This is a process of self-discovery. Your goal is to identify shifts in your worldview over time, but another equally important goal is to recognize moments of resilience in your history. You might not judge your actions or behaviors as misguided or even wrong or harmful but look for the strengths that got you through to today. What did you learn? Acknowledge that you survived; you are an overcomer, more than a conqueror.

You might journal about periods in your life. Write down how you saw the world when you were five years old, when you were ten, or fifteen, or twenty. Later, look back at your writing. What shifted? When did your belief about the world change?

Use this space to record your thoughts.

_____

_____

_____

_____

_____

_____

You can also turn to photographs for a visual timeline. If you do not have any, ask others who have known you at different periods of your life to share their photographs of you. Spread them out. Look at yourself over the years. What do you notice? When were you smiling and comfortable? When do you notice sparks of spontaneity? Which photos remind you of a sense of freedom you no longer have? When do you notice a shift in demeanor or a change in your eyes? Did your body change? Did you suddenly lose or gain weight over a short period? How did you place yourself in these photos? Were you engaged with the people around you, or did you pull away from them and stand in the background? Who was there with you at that time? Photos can offer many clues and point you to the years when your beliefs changed.

There are many ways to pinpoint the timeline of change, but before you start this work, prepare yourself. Remembering painful times can bring a sense of loss, as we already discussed, but also feelings of anger or sadness. Build a space for safety and support. It can be a space in your home or an imagined one. When building a safe place, you must take some time alone in silence and solitude and identify a real or imaginary place where you feel at peace and in tune with your inner spirit. You must go deep within yourself, where you will find safety. The same premise is true in an actual place; you should still feel connected with your inner spirit and an intense sense of peace.

Visualization is another tool that many use because you can employ it wherever you are. To begin, close your eyes and visualize a safe, calming space. It could be a tropical beach, a snow-covered forest, or somewhere in your home where you feel very comfortable. Imagine a sanctuary you can retreat to when the world becomes difficult. It can be a real place, like your grandmother's house when you were small, or a place of imagined peace and beauty somewhere in the universe. In your visualization, look around you. What surrounds you to make you feel safe? Are there photographs of loved ones or a cat purring on your knee? Do you hear the waves or smell the scent of soup on the stove? Make it real. Bring it to life in your mind. This is the place you will go to if you find yourself overwhelmed in your reflective practice. At any time in your inner work, you can stop the process and go to that safe place, that calming place.

_____

_____

_____

_____

_____

_____

Another option that you may find benefit in is physical activity like mindful walking. Begin by walking slowly and deliberately, focusing on the sensation and movement of each breath, and your surrounding environment. Pay attention to the sounds and scents in the air. As your body eases and your mind relaxes, turn your thoughts to the moments of change in your life. Let the rhythm of walking anchor you to the present moment while you reach back into your memory. You may want to use your phone to record your thoughts if you worry you will not remember key memories later. Before the end of your walk, return to the present and practice mindful walking again. Give yourself time to focus on your breath and your body and think about how you will care for yourself when you return home.

_____

_____

_____

_____

_____

_____

   If you find yourself in a situation where you become very overwhelmed, it's okay to pause your work to seek support. Turn to people you trust, or seek out support groups or therapists. If it becomes urgent and you feel like you are in crisis, you must call 911 or go to the nearest emergency room. We want to heal our wounds, not open them. There is time for self-care—know and embrace the call for you to step back, and then come back to this work later.

   I was journaling once about my sister Cecily and how I viewed her when I was four years old. She always took care of me whenever my mom was at work. In those hours, she took on the mothering role. When I got home from school, she made sure I changed out of my uniform, had a snack, and did my homework. In my journal, I wrote about how I love her for that. And then, my journal entry shows me beginning to ask the question, "Why?"

She shouldn't have to do that, I wrote. *Why does she have to do that? Where is my mother?*

As I wrote, my thoughts took on a life of their own. As an adult, I know the answers to those questions. Simply, my mother had to work. She had four children to raise, and she needed to work. But in my writing, I was not an adult. I was once again a little girl.

Well, why? Other mothers don't have to work like that.

My journaling was a process of self-discovery. It really helped me understand that four-year-old Karen, as much as she loved her sister, was really worried about feeling safe, and those emotions were rooted in the fact that my mother wasn't there. Journaling helped me realize that my mother's absence was connected to my sense of abandonment and rejection. The act of writing helped me uncover early beliefs that formed my reactions later.

Despite my early beliefs, I don't carry any ill will. I never blame my mother. She was a single mother, and she had to make sacrifices to be able to provide for us. Her hard work and sacrifice meant she did not just provide for us in a mediocre way. She sent all her children through private schools, from kindergarten to college. She worked hard and sacrificed her own personal life. She did it from a place of love, no matter what my four-year-old self felt. Forgiveness and empathy are key in releasing yourself from past pain. You must learn to forgive yourself and others and realize that many times, people are acting out of what they have experienced in the past. Just as you have a story and have been wounded, so have others.

Have you ever thought about when you might have hurt someone, and it had little to do with them but all to do with your past and how you were trying to navigate life?

Journaling brought me an internal shift. It helped me identify when my beliefs about the world changed. I could pinpoint a moment of transition in my life. That is what you will do, too.

However you choose to explore your timeline, look for the shifts and changes in your life. Pay attention to your feelings as they pass through you. Where do you become tearful? Is there a moment when you feel burdened or frayed? Do shame and guilt make an appearance? In your reflective inner work, your new understanding may come as a big aha moment or in a quiet sense of sadness. Give yourself the grace to experience your emotions, and then take note of them. Thank them for pointing out what you must pay attention to and let them move out of you. Go to your place of safety and security if you need to recover and take breaks if you need them.

When you review your timeline as a whole, be kind to your past self. How can you encourage the younger you? How can you speak life and hope? Be the advocate for the person you once were. Tell them you will be okay, that you are there for them. Take them to the safe place you visualized, and show them how they can rest there, too.

_____

_____

_____

_____

_____

_____

The journey you take to healing is not just about survival but about finding purpose and strength in the work you do to become free. When the apostle Paul spoke to Christians in Rome, he spoke of belief. "There is a future of glory," he told the people before him, "if you have faith." You can go through battle after battle and conquer the enemy, but there is more to living than that. We deserve more than mere survival. We want to have faith that our greatness is there, waiting for us.

Once you have your timeline in front of you—whether it is detailed in words, photos, or memories—extend that line into your future. Point it towards a place of peace, where you know your purpose and can navigate life's challenges without the struggles you face today. What do you want in your freedom from pain?

Your work

1. What did you see when you looked at the timeline of your life? Were you able to pinpoint when you accepted the lies? What changed for you then?
2. Strong emotions tell us something is important to us. What emotions are arising from your self-reflection, and what do they say about your values?
3. Your timeline begins in the past and points to your future. Describe the future you want to manifest.
4. What would help you to commit to the vision and hope for the future, even if the work ahead of you is challenging?

Use this space to record your thoughts.

PLACES OF WOUNDEDNESS

All things work together for the good...
—Romans 8:28 (CSB)

Y ou wake up from a nightmare, sweating. In the dream, you were stuck; you couldn't escape, and now, with fear still coursing through your body, you still feel trapped. At first, you laughed at the challenge. *A maze? It's simple to find your way out. Anyone can do it.* You had been confident, blasé, and you had not taken it seriously. But now, as you turn corner after corner, your self-assuredness dwindles, and you feel frustration coming over you.

The dream returns to you more clearly as your breath slows. In the maze, the walls around you grew higher each time you looked up.

You fall asleep and are again in the maze. You run but reach a dead end. You race back towards the new paths opening ahead, but they begin to look the same. Which way is out?

Soon, without a clear way forward, hopelessness sets in. You try to talk yourself down and rely on reason and problem-solving because you're intelligent, right? But there is unreasonable panic under the surface of your skin. You reach another dead end and question yourself again. *Why can't I do this?* You berate yourself. *Why am I making it so hard? Why can't I figure this out?*

Many of us know this feeling of being trapped when we are caught in a life pattern. It seems like there is no way out. You may have found yourself facing the same relationship difficulties over and over or repeating the same unhelpful behaviors that push people and opportunities away from you rather than bring them closer. You are trapped in the nightmare maze, but it is much more frustrating and painful to face in the light of day. Although facing your pain and repetitive non-productive patterns, you have to know that you have power over them. You do not have to continue on the path you have traveled in the past; you can choose another path. Once you embrace your inner power and realize that you are not the person you were in the past, you will understand that you can conquer your past. It is fear that holds us to our past. Much like bullies, our past seems bigger and more powerful than what it is in reality. You just have to face the bullies of your past and take control known that you have what you need inside to beat your past and release the chains that bind you. You might say that it is harder done than said but is it really? We make self-promises like that will never happen to me again and guess what it doesn't. Why not make the same type of self-promise that I will no longer be in bondage by my past?

Dominique is a successful business owner with a professional degree. Her fiancé uses language that hurts her.

"You're stupid," he tells her. "No one else would want you if you left me."

She knows she's not stupid, yet his words still hurt and anger her.

I asked Dominique, "Are you stupid?"

"No." She is certain.

Of course, she is not stupid. She could not run her business so successfully if she were. She is professionally qualified. She contributes financially to her household. Her reality doesn't support his statement. She should be proud of her abilities and success, and her worth should be clear to her. Yet there is a nagging part of her that agrees with her fiancé's words, and self-doubt is creeping into her days.

Why do these words affect her? Why does she stay with him? As outsiders, it is easy for us to see how her fiancé's behavior reflects his own insecurities, inadequacies, trauma, and pain, not her worth. She knows she shouldn't internalize these insults, but his words are confirming something she worries about. *Maybe I am not so smart after all. Maybe I am destined to spend the rest of my days alone if I leave him.* She is inside the maze, turning corners, seeking the right turn that will lead to a happy marriage with him.

I ask Dominique to examine why she reacts the way she does. If nothing in her reality supports his words, why do they still impact her? She must address these crucial questions to free herself from this maze.

I have met many people whose wounds are carved deeply from trauma, abuse, and neglect. These are people who have been harmed by negative words and unexpected circumstances, who have had their self-esteem torn away or their worst fears confirmed. I have met people who were told that what they feel and think doesn't matter. They are silenced through abuse or fear and intimidation. In my work, I meet people with trauma pushed back so far in their minds they can no longer see it; instead, the trauma is manifesting itself in behaviors and reactions that seem unexplainable. Their souls have been silenced. They walk through the maze of woundedness, looking for answers.

Most wounds are caused by some type of trauma. An emotional shock or an extremely distressing experience causes severe emotional wounds or bodily injury, both of which may have long-lasting psychological effects. When left untreated, these wounds can result in emotional and spiritual infections that will ultimately result in physical, emotional, and spiritual death. Trauma is unique to each person. What is traumatizing to one person may not be traumatizing to another. It has many faces, but the face of trauma is not *your* face; you are not the trauma that you have experienced.

We can be triggered in the present by our past trauma. The past becomes integrated into us, and we rely on it to tell us how to react when we are faced with threats or uncertainty. It makes some of us feel lost. We feel fear, doubt, anger, and sorrow like it is fresh. It can, such as in cases of sexual abuse, result in confusion, dysmorphia, or in feelings of worthlessness. Whatever form trauma takes for you, it is painful and confusing. We know our circumstances don't substantiate what we are experiencing, and yet we feel it anyway.

Our brains, doing what they are designed to do, have

created neural pathways. These pathways are usually helpful. They allow us to run our lives efficiently, for the most part. We can drive home without consulting a map, remember the birthdays of loved ones, and ride a bike. Our brain's pathways bring us incredible moments, where the smell of budding flowers in the backyard might evoke the memory of a summer wedding; in another person, the pattering of rain on the roof can elicit a sense of safety; for me, the sound of laughter at a family gathering brings me a sense of belonging, of peace and comfort.

But our brains also create pathways around adverse and traumatic events. When you are presented with difficulties or uncertainty, shame, criticism, negative feedback, or bad memories, your body acts quickly. Your limbic system is activated. It evaluates these events, and if it detects a threat, it cues your survival responses, the ones that prefer a well-worn path from brain to body. It's so efficient, you react in seconds, even milliseconds, before you have time to think about an alternative response.

Some pathways no longer serve us. They lead us to dead ends as we navigate the maze of our woundedness. We get turned around and cannot make the right decisions and choices. Our confidence and self-esteem become depleted, replaced by uncertainty or fear. Soon, our perception of our own abilities changes, and we see limits where there were few before. We act out in frustration or anger or retreat in silence. We do it over and over, lost in the maze. Your job now is to lay down new neural pathways so that your body no longer shortcuts to the places of woundedness.

We can make it through this maze, but we must first acknowledge that there are pathways that will lead us out and pathways that will lead us back.

In the previous chapter, I asked you to look back to what happened to you—to pin it to a timeline—but you must also look forward to the future where you will walk free of the chains you carry now. When we are triggered by events that are occurring here in the present, our responses are not based on what we're experiencing in the here and now; the past is integrated into that response. The key to moving forward is recognizing what triggers our poor responses, our unhelpful thinking, or our fears. You started this work already. It is through this process that you can confront the lies, identify the trauma, and begin to recognize the subconscious voice that is influencing your decisions and thoughts.

The goal is to get out of the maze. A maze is not

straightforward; you can expect to find yourself on paths that lead nowhere. If you encounter a dead end, it's OK. Just turn back. Keep moving. Understand that it's normal to face dead ends or failures—life is full of disappointments and challenges. But these setbacks don't define you nor do they mean there's no hope. You can successfully navigate through the maze when you realize that you can face these obstacles. You need not retreat to the place of woundedness again. As you uncover the details of your past timeline, you will reveal opportunities to change your future.

Your challenge now is to acknowledge your trauma for what it is. Something happened to you, and it is a part of you now, yes. It has shaped you, certainly, but it does not define who you are.

Use this space to record your thoughts.

People—their actions and words—have tried to take control and dominate your life. You can take it back, relying on the strengths you developed from these experiences. What has made you strong and victorious is enduring the events that have happened to you, including the traumas, and they are now in the past.

Begin by acknowledging your pain. Self-reflection can be uncomfortable, especially when it uncovers wounds we would rather not acknowledge. You cannot continue to live in this pain. Build a future where you have ownership of your life. This takes courage, persistence, and honest self-evaluation. Document what happened to you but also acknowledge the strengths that helped you survive. Conduct an inventory of the wisdom and skills you have on hand to help you change.

I like to think about the apostle Paul's letter to the Corinthians. In it, Paul defends his ministry against accusations and challenges. Doubt can overtake us, he says, but we really must be disciplined in our thinking, "[taking] captive every thought to make it obedient to Christ" (2 Corinthians 10:5 NIV). Consider where you want to be and stay focused. Challenge yourself to remain committed to your journey, and don't let fear cause you to turn back.

It's also crucial to challenge your negative

self-perceptions. You can replace them and bring them under control with positive views. It's spiritual warfare, so to speak, and you are saving your soul from the lies told to you in the past. Negative self-perceptions like no one loves me, I am invisible and don't have a voice worth hearing, I'm not good enough, I will never be happy or loved, and I am all alone in this world. You know them because you have the same recordings playing in your head.

The human brain is active. Over the course of a day, we use one hundred billion neurons to power seventy thousand thoughts, more than forty every minute. Ninety-five percent of these thoughts are repetitive. As a result, we want to be very intentional about what we allow to penetrate our thoughts. Our minds cannot focus on many things at once, so your job now is to remain focused on healing and life so that your mind has fewer resources to respond to threats.

Challenge the harmful thoughts. When negative thinking—thoughts based on doubt, shame, fear, guilt—are circling in your mind, you must challenge your thoughts by asking, "Does this thought have any value? Is it life-giving?" If it isn't, you don't need it. You must say to yourself: "I don't live in the past anymore. I don't have to live in the oppression of these thoughts."

Condemnation in your thoughts takes energy away from you and stops you from moving forward. With negative thinking, we embrace our woundedness and permit our minds and bodies to respond to events as threats. We react, and it affects the people around us.

If you think:	Then say:
Nobody loves me.	*It's not true. I am lovable.*
Nobody cares.	*You're taking it to an extreme. There are people who care about me.*

Guard your heart. Protect yourself. Challenge your thinking. If a thought isn't life-giving or valuable, recognize that you don't need to engage with it. If you believe it is worth questioning further for personal growth, however, ask yourself, *Why am I thinking this way?* Probe the reasons you might accept negative thinking in your life.

Over the next week, I encourage you to undertake a reflective activity. Pay close attention to what people around you are saying and doing, and take note of how these interactions impact you. Be deliberate in this observation. Each day, consider the thoughts you're allowing to take hold. Challenge yourself: *Are these thoughts life-giving? Are they constructive and beneficial to my well-being?* Attention to thoughts and interactions can be somewhat of a push and pull. When paying attention to your thoughts, you explore your inner feelings, emotions, memories, and reflections. Attending to your interactions is focusing on the outer world, being actively aware of the conversation, non-verbal clues, and your response to the environment. This week-long exercise in mindfulness and introspection will help you better understand and manage the influences shaping your mindset.

This reflection might lead you back to a trauma or a past wound. When you identify such a thought, remind yourself that it stems from a place you no longer reside in. Reassure yourself with a statement of fact: *I don't live there anymore.* Free yourself from the oppression of those thoughts, from the pain and wounds of the past, because you have moved beyond that place. Make sure that the words you speak about yourself, and your circumstances are lined up with life-giving thoughts.

Use this space to record your thoughts.

_____

_____

_____

_____

_____

_____

Engage in life-affirming thoughts. Research has shown that self-criticism changes our brains and so does positive self-talk. Negative self-talk is normal, but when done regularly, it can nudge you towards perfectionism and comparison with others, which diminishes self-love and acceptance. Positive self-talk improves our focus. We use our words to heal:

I am not my mistakes.
I am in charge of how I see myself.
I am my own support system.
I am enough, just as I am, with what I have.
My ability to overcome challenges is immense.
My resilience has carried me through difficult times.

We know the power of words—we came to believe the lies spoken over us, didn't we? So, in our quest to escape the maze of woundedness, we must speak to ourselves with kindness, care, and concern. Research shows that over time, affirmations decrease stress and create new neural pathways. On my path of continual healing, I focus on how God sees me, which builds my self-confidence and internal peace even when I am faced with life challenges and ill-willed people. I choose to believe the truth rather than a lie.

_____

_____

_____

_____

_____

_____

Place accountability where it belongs. What happened to you was a moment in time, an experience that you had. It doesn't define who you are, what you were created to be, or what you will be in the future. If someone hurts you, intentionally or not, are you responsible for their actions? No. You are not responsible for the choices they make. If someone rejects you, it doesn't mean there's something wrong with you; it is simply their choice. If your father was emotionally unavailable—even if he was physically present—it doesn't mean there was something wrong with you. Accountability must rest with him. The choices people make reflect where they are in their own development, and they may be in the maze of woundedness, too. Their behaviors or choices shouldn't be interpreted as a reflection of your worth. "It's not what goes into a man but what comes out," Jesus told the Pharisees. External trauma does not define your identity; it's your inner resilience and strength that matters.

What you are responsible for is how you move forward with this knowledge. You can ask, "Why am I perceiving it this way? Why is it making me feel this way? Why am I responding in this way if it is not about me?" For instance, if someone's words make you feel inadequate, it's not their words that you should analyze but why those words trigger feelings of inadequacy in you. If you can't figure it out right away or if it doesn't resonate immediately, set it aside. It will come back when you're ready as part of your healing process.

Dominique, by examining her timeline, is beginning to understand where her woundedness lies. It is not necessarily in her relationship with her fiancé. In her counseling sessions, I witness her work her way through the maze. She is looking for the pathway that will get her to the other side where her woundedness will be healed. She is being triggered in the present by something from her past, and her reactions and feelings towards her fiancé's verbal abuse are reasonable. But why does she let his disparaging words affect her so deeply when they are not true?

We examined it more closely to understand where and when she was first wounded. Dominique tells me she is particularly hurt when she feels her fiancé withholding his love. As she explores this painful feeling, she begins to see a pattern she recognizes from her childhood. When she upset her mother, she explains, her mother would ignore her. She realizes what she learned from this: Love comes with pain. Now, when her partner withholds affection or speaks harshly, she feels the way she did as a child. To avoid the pain, she finds herself trying to do things to stop him from acting in this way, which keeps her in the relationship. She's seeking to make him love her. However, what he offers isn't really love. It's not just unwillingness to love; due to his own wounds, he's unable to show love.

"It's a pattern," she tells me, with realization. She attracts people who are unable to love her, and she makes a futile attempt to make them love her.

If someone loves you, they don't constantly belittle you or do things that are physically and emotionally hurtful or harmful, as Dominique's fiancé does. Yet many of us have come to believe lies like this. We have normalized struggles in our lives. Everything does not have to be a struggle. Good does not have to come with pain. Love does not have to come with hurt. In fact, when someone loves you, they cherish you, and they treat you well. They don't hurt you. They don't say things to you that are belittling and damaging consistently. But when we begin to expect that, we accept it in our relationships and in the circumstances of our lives.

Dominique sees now that the path out of the maze is not the one she was looking for; it is one that will give her freedom from the lies that have told her she must struggle, even in love.

You are dreaming about the maze again. This time, when you wake up from the nightmare, you tell yourself to return to sleep. You want to go back to the world of dreams and to the maze. Now that you have had a moment to breathe and to think, you can draw on your courage. Yes, you'll need to be vigilant. Yes, you will need to rely on all the wisdom you gained from your mistakes, but you are ready to take responsibility for finding your way out.

You know you aren't to blame for getting stuck—the pathways were designed to confuse you. But you can't stop when there is a dead end. There is a way out. You must keep moving and rely on your strengths. You know this isn't a maze problem—you were sent off-course by what happened to you. Your fears are based on someone else's idea of you.

Now, you will guard your heart with diligence, as Proverbs 4:23 urges us to do, because out of it comes all life.

Your work

1. What dead ends do you find yourself running into over and over?

2. Sift through the feelings associated with these dead ends. Why were you returning to what was familiar? What feelings did you encounter? Are those feelings connected to another time when you first felt that way?

3. What are your positive characteristics? What are your accomplishments?

4. When you hear negative thoughts or words, write down the opposite. Look at them and ask which you would rather embrace. Which would you rather be your reality, in the present and the future?

Use this space to record your thoughts.

_____

_____

_____

_____

_____

_____

_____

Chapter 7

YOU CAN BE FREE

I press toward the mark for the prize of the high calling...

—Philippians 3:14 (WEB)

As a psychologist, I am fortunate to witness people undergo transformation. I see their sense of excitement grow as they move towards something more significant than they expected. I see their dreams and desires manifesting when they are no longer bound by fear, shame, and self-blame. I see self-forgiveness. Where before they had to protect themselves and stay vigilant, now they become more open and vulnerable. I see their hard shells begin to soften. They begin to see themselves through a different lens as their worldview shifts.

III

This is a critical period of transformation. It is thrilling, and yet we feel trepidation as we look down our future path. What will we find when we go forth? We must live in the present and focus on what is ahead. Like an Olympic runner, we cannot look backward; it will slow us down. The prize is ahead of us.

Returning to old habits, routines, or behaviors is not a failure. It is a chance to remind yourself what is important to you. Stepping forward again is progress, and each time you do it, you will become more confident. I call this the progression of freedom—each time you make progress; you feel more internal peace. You become open to love.

Unbinding yourself from the chains of old hurts is bringing you closer to freedom. You will exit the maze and see you have become someone stronger and greater. Once you have acknowledged that the responsibility for the actions of others belongs to them, not to you, the chains pressing down on you will feel lighter, and you will be able to hear over their rattle for the first time in a long time.

Your vision will become keener. You will see life and yourself with a more transparent lens. You will see the light, positive, nurturing side of life. As you step forward towards freedom, little by little, anxiety will be lifted as will depression, distress, uncertainty, shame, and fear.

Letting go and exploring the unfamiliar paths in front of you may be scary—it's not the pain you are familiar with—and this new sense of movement can make you feel fearful or unconfident. Be aware of these emotions and allow them to be present, but acknowledge you are now greater than they are. Refuse to regress. Freedom is about liberation. It's living without being dominated. You will earn the ability to go beyond the limits previously set out for you, but freedom also goes beyond the physical and mental realms. It is where you can see your purpose and connect to awe, delight, and the vastness of possibility.

Astronauts talk about the transformative experience of seeing Earth for the first time from space. It is called the Overview Effect. When they reach space after years of intense training and the momentous pressure of a safe liftoff, they see Earth across such a great distance that a cognitive shift occurs. They see the world and themselves suddenly with awe and a sense of cosmic connection. It changes how they see themselves and how they see earthly problems. Some describe it as profoundly trans-formative thanks to the overwhelming emotion evoked by this global view.

We can't all go to space, but the work we do to understand our pain and to free ourselves from it—and to acknowledge our role in perpetuating it even if we aren't responsible for its cause—is the effort of astronauts. We are in training, learning the mechanical systems and necessary routines that will launch us beyond our current reality. We press towards this destination; the prize is a new perspective on our pain. We will see our past and our purpose newly.

I felt this shift acutely one morning, when I woke up thinking about my father. My father did not raise me. He was not a part of my life. In fact, in my lifetime, I have seen him only four times. I never had any ill will towards him because my mother never spoke negatively about him, but I did not feel a sense of love or connectedness. However, as I freed myself from the chains of my pain, the sense of freedom brought me something unexpected: an overwhelming sense of love towards my father. *Love.*

I marveled at this revelation. I felt a physical sense of love the same way I loved my mother for her constant presence and sacrifices. Even though he was absent, I realized he played an essential and integral role in my life. He gave me *life.* Without him, I would not have that. I understood that the mere fact of him giving me life meant he played a role in my greatness.

The sense of peace and love I felt towards my father once I saw him in his purest form was unexpected. How could I love someone who had not been part of my life? How could I feel such gratitude? Yet he had played a significant role in my existence, and I could love him for that.

Wow, I thought. *Where did this come from?* I could see him, for the first time, without pain impeding my view. And that's when I realized this realization came from being free. I could connect to my father beyond the facts and events of my life. I had a new understanding of the message of 1 Peter 4:8: "Above all, have fervent and unfailing love for one another, because love covers a multitude of sins [it overlooks unkindness and unselfishly seeks the best for others]" (AMP).

I call this work dancing with the pain. As you propel yourself towards freedom, you develop a new relationship with your past. It is not as painful as you experienced it before. It doesn't have an impact like it once did. You may wake one day, as I did, and see the value in it, the lightness of it, and the other side. You can talk about it without becoming overwhelmed or distressed; you are no longer embodied in the pain. It is outside of you.

As you acclimate to this new environment of freedom and the lightness of your body and mind absent of chains, you begin taking the lead. You determine how the dance will flow. Your pain is a part of your past but no longer has power over you, your thoughts, decisions, and especially your happiness and future. You determine the rest of your story, which is the best of your story. You no longer feel forced to put its weight on your waist or your arm. You have a choice. You can decide the dance moves. You can change the dance or choose another partner.

When you dance, life becomes more joyful and free. You might even find laughter. You must welcome laughter, even in times of confusion or grief. Laughter is healing. I know this personally as I heal from the passing of my mother. Despite my grief, I now laugh at some of the things she did. Although I miss her greatly, I see who she was and understand that all is well with her as she has completed her purpose for being in this realm and can rest and enjoy eternity with joy. I see it now with a different lens. I no longer have the dry bones of sorrow described by Proverbs 17:22; I take the good medicine of laughter. This is the dance. Pain and grief may return, but we can dance with it from a new position and perspective. We dance because it is growth, and it leads to freedom.

People will notice when you move into freedom. They will sense your purpose. Some of them will want you to look back. They will try to deflect your attention from the road ahead of you. They will tell you that freedom is not the prize. They will blame and shame you for leaving them behind, cutting ties, or setting boundaries. They will tell you that you don't appreciate everything they have done for you.

There will be times when your pain and hurt return, when old thoughts and beliefs try to hold you back once more. What initially appears tempting or safe might ensnare you in your old life or mindset. You may grieve the loss of what you knew or feel unsettled by the uncertainty of the future. You might encounter trauma you haven't yet fully healed from. This is when you must remember to pause and breathe; you want to remember your vision of freedom.

When I worked in foster care, I saw how fearful people could be when faced with uncertainty, even when the reward was great. Once, I met a parent who had lost her child to the system. Amber loved her child, and she was doing everything she could to get her child back from foster care. She understood that her behavior had led to the removal of her child, and now she was working hard to turn her life around and to show she could successfully parent her child. It took a long time, and a few years passed without reunification, but Amber showed dedication and grit. She completed all required parenting classes, attended therapy addressing the reason for child welfare involvement, and was secure, employed, and maintained regular visitation with her child, showing she could offer age-appropriate activities and use age-appropriate parenting strategies. It was promising. But when the time got close to her child being returned to her, Amber self-sabotaged her progress and lost the chance for reunification.

Amber tried again, but she could not find her way to freedom from the lies that bound her. Just as the reunification date came near, it happened again: she returned to her old behaviors and lost another chance to parent her child.

I knew Amber could parent her child and provide a good home. She had done the hard work of change and showed such commitment. But each time she faced the prospect of her renewed responsibilities, fear crept in. She believed the voices that said, *You can't do anything right; you are a terrible person and a worse parent.* When she listened to these voices, she worried she wouldn't be able to parent her child in the way she hoped, and they wouldn't meet the system's expectations, but most importantly, she worried she wouldn't be able to do so on her own. If she failed, she would have to face the removal of her child again. It was easier to fall back on old habits and behaviors and avoid the pain altogether.

It was easier to face the disappointment than to face the fear.

Self-sabotage is not unusual when we get a glimpse of the freedom ahead of us. It's easier to turn back to what we know and what is familiar when the tentacles of fear reach for us. We have built habits and coping strategies around old problems and traumas; we have set up patterns and routines to support the lives we know, even if those patterns and routines have bound us to the pain we no longer want. It is when we feel the fear that we must be bravest and dig deep into ourselves for strength. We must dance with the pain.

Use this space to record your thoughts.

_____

_____

_____

_____

_____

_____

_____

_____

An octopus is a wondrous creature, one rarely met. A woman walking the shoreline in Victoria, British Columbia, Canada, however, unexpectedly befriended one. One day, standing at the shore, she leaned over to look into the water. An octopus, fearful of how close the woman was to it, wrapped its tentacles around the woman's ankles. The woman was caught by surprise. But when the octopus began tightening its grip around her legs, the woman became terrified. Its grip clamped tighter, and she feared for her life.

The octopus refused to let go. Its grip was strong. The woman could not move.

Then, she realized she had some power, even if she couldn't escape. She forced herself to relax and breathe deeply.

She breathed. She waited.

Sensing the change in her, the octopus realized the woman was not a threat after all and released her.

When our bodies face fear, our instinct is to freeze or take flight. Sometimes, we fight. But I'm here to tell you, you don't have to go backward into these responses. If you become ensnared by fear, take a moment. This is only a test of your commitment to your authentic self.

Fight against the instinct to panic when the tentacles

of past pain reach for you. Reassure yourself that you know what to do. You won't feel the torment that you felt before. You may feel irritated, agitated, or even angered about it, but no torment. You can tell yourself to relax and breathe until the tentacles release you.

Yes, if you step backward, you will need to navigate the maze to freedom again, but here is the good news: now, you know the way. You can find the exit again. You see what is beyond it, and you know that if you persevere, you can enjoy freedom again. The paths look familiar, and you know which landmarks will lead you to freedom.

When you can do this, you've made the paradigm shift.

We cannot walk the new path of freedom alone. You will need support, but your job now as you enter freedom is to disengage from unhealthy relationships and patterns. It is hard, and you will experience feelings of loss or guilt. People who supported you in your old life might be angry; others will try to pull you back. They are afraid of being alone in a life bound by pain, and because you have shown them that freedom is possible, they will be fearful that they must change, too. Change brings uncertainty, and you can be sympathetic to their fear. But you must look forward to your new life and the greatness in front of you. They will need to walk the maze as you did. Your role in their lives is different now; your role is to inspire hope, and you must move forward and let them follow. You cannot remain entangled in negativity or toxic relationships.

As the parameters of your freedom grow, you can reach back and grab the hand of others struggling with their woundedness and show them the way. But now, you must become comfortable with your new perspective and growth. The sun is rising; it is time to lift off and aim for the other shore. to become comfortable with your new perspective and growth. You are the eagle soaring and embracing your life of freedom and purpose, learning to breathe air for the first time after most of your life underwater. The sun is rising; it is time to lift off and aim for the other shore. The eagle is known for its keen eyesight and expansive wings representing freedom, transcendence, and power.

But must I do this alone? You wonder. No. Now, you need a community to nurture your freedom. Turn to the people who helped you navigate the maze, to the friends, therapists, and supporters who held onto hope for you when you were feeling lost. They will be your companions now. Grow your community and find like-minded people who are positive and non-judgmental, who will be honest yet kind and who are "for" you. They will help you rely on what you learned already.

See and experience freedom. Grow into it. Because of your pain, you are strong. You have what you need now. Say it aloud: *I was prepared for this.*

You survived the pain. You can survive freedom.

Your work

1. You have new wings. You can suddenly fly to a place where you have a new perspective. What does it look like from here? What will you rest your vision on?

2. As you emerge into freedom, who is your community? Are there relationships that you find to be more nurturing? Who can help you build freedom?

3. Can you give yourself permission to release yourself from relationships that no longer support you? What do you need to do to disengage? Do you need to set new boundaries or exit the relationship?

4. You are in a dance with old pain. How can you lead the dance toward freedom?

Use this space to record your thoughts.

Chapter 8

THE PURPOSE IN THE PAIN

And the peace of God, which transcends all understanding, will guard your hearts and your minds...
—Philippians 4:7 (NIV)

Emotional and spiritual freedom gives you a quality of life you cannot find in pain. You no longer need to run after things that distract you and fill the holes in your soul. You move towards your greatness and fill yourself with love and peace. You engage with other humans in a new way as part of a greater community. You see a movement towards your purpose.

In his poem "Le Train de ma Vie," Jean D'Ormesson says, Life is a train journey. When we climb on board, we meet the people who will travel with us for a time:

our parents, siblings, colleagues, and the ones we will fall in love with. The voyage will be full of hellos, good-byes, and farewells. Each of us is scheduled to get off at an unknown station. Some departures will leave us feeling great loss; at other times, people will leave so quietly that we will not even notice. The journey brings joy, pain, expectations, and loss.[3]

In D'Ormesson's view, because we share our journey with others, we are responsible for leaving only beautiful memories. Yet, realistically, we know our journey is not entirely pleasurable. We share it with people who are in pain and passengers who crowd our space with their hurt, and though they may not be on board for long, they leave lasting reminders. We make many more stops before we can leave the memory of them behind. Some-times, we are the ones in pain, sharing it with others.

The journey makes us expectant. We watch the hori-zon for our destination. Expectations, D'Ormesson points out, are a part of life. They push us towards decisions that alter our lives. Some of the wickedness in our world happens because people expect something from someone else, and when they don't get it, they be-come angry. It is like road rage. If a driver cuts in front of another in traffic, the other driver could interpret it as intentional and retaliate aggressively. We expect

3. D'Ormesson, J, (2009). Le train del ma vie [The Train of Life].

people to think about their effect on us, and when they hurt us or offend us, we take on the hurt or offense. We can easily become the ones who hurt or offend in this state of mind.

If you have been working towards freedom with me, lifting off the chains that bind you to pain, you can see now that when someone treats you poorly, their actions do not reflect who you are. They are acting out of their own pain, and their actions reflect the turmoil inside their hearts and what happened to them.

Now, with freedom and lightness, you are moving forward. Your journey continues, and while you still travel with some familiar passengers, others are coming aboard, bringing possibility, hope, and optimism. It is time for you to look towards the horizon. Your purpose is becoming clearer.

When we are bound in chains and wrap our minds with the lies others spoke over us, we see life through a narrow lens. When we break free from the chains and release the lies, our vision is widened—our perception changes. We dance with our pain and step towards freedom. That's what I did as I broke loose from the death grip of my chains. What I learned was this: In freedom, you can let life unfold and be at peace with it. You reach a point where you no longer have to fight, and it is a glorious thing.

I was in my late thirties, still trying to figure life out why things were happening the way they were. I was making decisions and mistakes based on my pain and fear, rather than making decisions based on a mindset of grace and giving people the benefit of doubt. I was very angry and would lash out with mean-spiritedness if I thought they were doing something to me. *You won't hurt me*, was my attitude. I thought if I didn't take care of myself, no one else would. That wasn't true, but I just had to fight. But how can you live if you're always fighting?

This attitude, my approach to life back then, did not allow me to develop true friendships. It did not allow me to have true emotional intimacy in marriage. I hid behind a mask. I wore it to protect myself, showing the person, I thought I should be. Looking back, I realize this mask caused me to compromise some of my morals in order to feel better.

At one point during this time, early in my career, I worked for a daycare run by Catholic nuns. It was clear they didn't want me there, but I had been hired by the Board, so they had little say in the decision. Instead, they tried to make it uncomfortable for me with sabotaging behaviors and accusations. It became so overwhelming that I found it a constant struggle just to do my job.

They brought me before the Board, and I was asked to attend a meeting to respond to the accusations.

But the man who hired me, Walter, was very supportive of me and my work. Before we joined the meeting with the nuns, he told me, "When we go into this meeting, just relax. You don't have to prove anything to anyone. Be open. Hear what they say. If you have a response, you can give that, but you don't have to justify what you're doing."

We heard the point of view of the nuns, and I heard them lie and say all sorts of horrible things about me. But Walter's encouragement helped me let the negative energy flow around me. I didn't own it, I realized. I didn't have to internalize their accusations. I didn't need to defend myself or fight back. I knew what I was doing was right. I didn't have to fight a fight. Because there was no fight, it was a struggle they created amongst themselves.

Nonetheless, it was very stressful. I had to sit there and remain calm despite how difficult it was.

"Mmm-hmm. I see. OK," I said in response to their statements.

When it got really, really difficult, Walter would just tap my knee as if to say, *Hey, it's OK. You don't have to say anything.*

I could have been angry. Instead, I remained open.

And then they began to tell on themselves. When

questioned, the nun's version of events was different from that of the parents and staff. Their version aligned with what I presented before entering the meeting. I had to push back my initial instinct to protect myself and allow the matter to play out, which was not my usual stance. I was used to fighting and engaging in struggle.

The Board could see what they were saying was not true, and they decided in my favor. The nuns were told to back off and let me do my job.

Walter's advice helped me through that trial, and I learned something that day. I could choose not to struggle.

Five or six years later, I found myself in another meeting where my work was being called into question. An older, long-standing employee didn't like me and was pulling rank. A mediation session to resolve the dispute was scheduled, and as the meeting began, Walter's words came to me. *You don't have to defend yourself*, he reminded me. *Let her speak. Be open. You don't have to justify yourself just because someone asks you to.*

I sat there, open, and at peace. It was not my problem to hold; it was hers.

Like before, I saw the woman begin to tell on herself.

She became angry when I wouldn't engage, even when I responded with accountability, saying, "You know what? I can understand that, and I'll work on that." But I refused to take on her anger and return it to her.

She wanted conflict, and when I didn't participate, she became frustrated. She was nearly fired because she became belligerent.

The earlier situation with the nuns had been difficult, but it had prepared me for this new challenge. This time, when I did not have anybody to sit with me and encourage me, I was able to utilize the skills I had developed. So even though Walter wasn't there with his reminders in the second go-round, I was able to tap my own knee and carry forward what I learned.

A lot of times, before we find freedom, we're fighting for something. Or about something. Or against something. I was. When you choose not to fight, it doesn't mean that you've surrendered. It means you are okay with who you are. Freedom means you no longer base your idea of yourself on someone else's view, whether it is accolades or insults; you see yourself free of all of it. It becomes easier to be genuine and authentically you. You can remove the mask you wore for so long.

In the end, that is the purpose of the pain—to finally reveal yourself. You feel a sense of solace and live in faith that it will work out, even when there is struggle. You can look at some of your most painful memories and say, "That's okay," because those moments led you to the individual you are, to your greatness. Pain is a catalyst, and like love, it combusts under pressure to move us forward in our journey.

Use this space to record your thoughts.

_____

_____

_____

_____

_____

_____

There comes a point in your journey to freedom when you begin to realize how far you have come. Even when it seemed doubtful, your destination was nearing.

You begin to see how other people carry pain. You see how they attach to mindsets and situations that perpetuate their pain. The more we become free of our own pain, the easier it is to see in others—and we learn not to judge them.

Growing up, I always saw myself as being tolerated. I felt I lived in the shadow of others, especially my sister Cecily. She never said or did anything to make me feel that way. I think it was more how other adults treated me; it seemed clear that she was the one they wanted there, and I was invited because I was her younger sister and that was the right thing to do, right? Cecily was and still is outgoing and seems to have so much fun. I compare her to the Energizer Bunny. Through the course of my life, I picked up on the reactions of others to her infectious spirit, and I interpreted those as statements of my own worth.

Once, I was asked to attend a meeting on behalf of the church I went to as a child and teen. It was a significant meeting. I had prepared a proposal for our church requesting funding for its daycare center, and the priest and I were to meet a high state official to discuss our request. The priest and I had collaborated on the proposal, and we spoke a number of times, swapping emails back and forth. I was pleased to be asked to join him and proud to be there.

My sister wasn't involved in this project, but the priest knew her well. She attended Mass each week, and her enthusiasm made her memorable. Still, it hurt me when, during introductions, the priest introduced me to the state official as "Cecily's sister." He had forgotten my name. I felt invisible, and it reinforced my idea of myself. In my eyes, I was overlooked once again. Here I was, an adult, standing in the shadows.

The official was kind. Perhaps he had felt the same way at some point in his life. He turned to me and smiled, "Is that her name? 'Cecily's Sister'?" He didn't give the priest time to respond and said, "Young lady, what's your name?"

This kind man understood kinship, and he wasn't

going to allow me to remain in the shadows. He reached into the dim light and pulled me out. I smiled and thanked the State Representative. I felt the bright light that was immediately dimmed when I heard the words "This is Cecily's sister" began to illuminate in my heart; at that moment, I knew that I was seen and could shine in my unique greatness in confidence.

In reality, I was never in Cecily's shadow. People see her and say, "Oh, she is outgoing and free-spirited." The world needs people like her. As I moved towards my own greatness, I realized I didn't have to be outgoing like her to be seen. There is value in both of us, even if we approach the world differently. If you can't see me, you're blind to this possibility, not me.

Over time, I rewrote my story, and while the pain was still part of it, it was no longer the reason for it. Today, I see a person who once questioned her value, a person who has struggled to feel connected and wanted. Looking back, I see now that the hurtful things people said were a result of their ignorance, inconsideration, or fallibility. How I saw myself was as much what was said to me as what I let myself continue to believe.

In time, as I worked on finding freedom from my own chains, my vision became clearer in other areas of my life. Possibility became reality. This book is a possibility manifested—not just for me to tell my story but to guide others in their journey of healing and becoming free from their pain and the chains that bind them.

You can help someone else be free. Like the state official who asked me my name, like Walter, you can reach back and let someone else know you see their struggle for self-actualization and purpose. You can walk beside others who are emerging into their authentic self.

Your work

1. What does freedom feel like to you? What is the place of peace you seek?
2. What do you need to feel free?
3. Are you afraid of the unknowns of freedom?
4. What are your expectations of freedom?
5. Look in the mirror. What do you see? Are you still on the journey towards freedom, or do you see yourself already there?
6. Rewrite your story so that pain is part of it, not the reason for it. Then, review your work. Are you still attached to your pain?

Use this space to record your thoughts.

Chapter 9

TRAUMA TO TRIUMPH:
LIVING OUT YOUR DIVINE PURPOSE

Before I formed you in the womb I knew you [and approved of you as My chosen instrument], And before you were born, I consecrated you [to Myself as My own].

—Jeremiah 1:5 (AMP)

Your purpose is bigger than you. It is bigger than your natural experience. It makes itself known through your journey towards freedom, and it will bring meaning to your days. You will discover gifts within you that connect you to others.

Years ago, when I was young, I used to love to fight. I would fight anybody—male, female, grown person, little person, it didn't matter. I had no fear. If I saw someone being picked on, I would jump in where most people would just walk away. I'd say, "You leave them alone!" and get in the middle. I'd push. I'd throw fists. Sometimes, I would find myself in a full-blown fistfight with people I didn't even know.

My sister, once, tried to jump in and protect me from an older boy, and the bully hit her in the chest.

"I don't need your help!" I shouted at her then threw myself at the older boy again because he hit her.

If there was someone to defend, I got tangled up in the fight.

As I grew into adulthood, my urge to physically fight diminished, but if I saw someone mistreating another person, I would jump in to verbally defend the underdog. If someone could not defend or help themselves, I made it my business to be there. I learned, eventually, to use my voice, to be forceful and say, "No, you're not doing that to me." I had a right to use my voice to advocate for myself.

At one point, as I unbound myself from my chains and separated the lies from the truth, I began to consider what it was that urged me to jump into a tussle without fear. It wasn't like I came from a family of bullies or fighters. Yet, there was something in me that *liked* to fight. What was the purpose in my desire to fight for someone else?

Over time, I realized that desire really derived from a

spiritual source. It was the same source that supported me in prayer for others in need of strength. When I pray, I fight for them in prayer. Was this urge to fight really a calling to be a spiritual warrior? Perhaps I had heard my calling already as that young person, but without the experience of life behind me, and believing the lies that were spoken over me, I misinterpreted the message.

Gradually, I found myself praying for people and travailing for people, doing what I call *spiritual warfare*. When people need prayer, I fight. Not with my fists anymore, but on a spiritual level. Scripture tells us we fight not against flesh and blood, but against powers, principalities, people in high places, and I do. Fighting, I see now, is really part of my purpose. I protect and fight for people who feel the way I felt at one time: undefended, left to protect myself, with no one to speak up for me. My fight was fought alone, or so I thought. But my pain led me to my real purpose, and now in my counseling practice, I am an advocate so people know they have a defender, a compassionate supporter, someone who will champion their cause. The purpose in my pain has been revealed to me in so many ways. It has come full circle.

The true shift towards my freedom probably happened after my mother died. I watched her try to let go of all the pain she still held within herself in her transition into death. She struggled at the end with some very deep-rooted hurts. Whenever she got really sick, she would talk about her mother not wanting her. That troubled her to the end. "Why didn't she love me?" she asked. The pain of abandonment, long-held, lived long in her, and because of it, she was afraid to be loved—because if your mother can discard you, then who can you trust? I am sure that there was a logical and maybe even a loving and compassionate reason my grandmother sent my mother to live with her great-aunt shortly after her birth. It was the reason, I believe, that my mother promised herself to always keep her children with her, even when it was hard. It is probably why she never married and why she never wanted anyone to have a say over her children. Imagine the beauty in life that she missed because of the unreconciled pain.

I watched her grapple with these old wounds, with what she thought was her hidden sadness, and I came to believe that we have to release ourselves from our pain in this world—to find a place where we truly remember who we are in order to grasp onto the next without struggle. *Lord*, I prayed, watching my mother, *whatever my issues are, whatever they may be, even those that I am not aware of today, please allow me to work through them and to be free and healed from them so that when it's time for me to leave this life I can do it in peace, with no struggle, and so those I leave behind can be at peace with my passing because I live and love in peace.*

When our woundedness no longer clouds our vision, we remember who we are spiritually. I think that's the triumph of freedom for me. I understand now that we are, beyond our human experiences, spiritual beings wrapped in a physical flesh and having a "soulish" experience. Here in this world, though, we tend to think that what we experience in our humanness is who we are. But that's not it. Once we come to terms with that and understand that we are truly *spirit*, these challenges we encounter become detached from us, and we can let them go. What I did is okay. And what I didn't do, it is okay. The connection between me and my creator is the gift.

For me, the purpose of the pain is being able to look at my life and see that it has been touched by many people. There is a connection. I can reach back into my memory without pain, and I can reach forward to connect with others who need guidance on their path to freedom.

I want you to continue the work you began here. It must carry forward. Self-realization is not a process that ends; your growth will continue as you work towards freedom and discover the purpose in your pain.

What is the purpose in your pain? The answer is inside of you. That is where you must search inside of you. You can't find peace in material things. You can't find peace in accolades or awards because these can come and can go. True peace is from inside, but it comes with effort.

In your work to unbind yourself from your chains, you may find you become sensitive and aware of the pain of others. Your compassion will grow for others and for yourself. It will fortify the roots of your purpose, which stands like a tree. When the purpose in your pain is unknown, your roots are not deep enough. As the tree grows and is nourished, the roots will grow deeper and stronger to keep you standing when storms come, so you're not blown to the ground. You may sway back and forth and bend with the wind, but you will not break. Continue this work until you find your purpose. It is there, waiting for you to break free of the lies holding you to a life where you are dissatisfied and unfulfilled. Your tree of purpose will grow. It will move and flow with the winds of life. You will feel its strength inside of you.

Now, having worked through my pain and lifted off the chains that bound me to it, I am living in freedom, pursuing my purpose. But my life is shifting again, and I don't know what to expect from the years ahead. The purpose in the pain really is to connect you back to the core of who you are. My purpose is illuminating as I experience growth and healing. Before, I believed my purpose was to be a psychologist. Then, I saw that it was to be an advocate. Now, my purpose is becoming even clearer. I understand I am an emotional and spiritual healer and teacher. I want people to walk without their pain, to help them move from one stage to the next. I see God bringing people to me with this message of purpose. "Psychologist" is, I see now, a job title. Advocacy is how I carry out my purpose. I continue to grow and change. I remind myself of the words in Ecclesiastes: There is a season and a time. This is true for every purpose.

Recently, I visited my great-aunt, Hilda. Aunt Hilda is a small woman of medium build, with a caramel complexion. The starched crease in her pants spoke of the care she puts into a family visit. I looked around her tidy living room, noticing the mementos and photographs on display. A photo on the mantel caught my eye. In it, there was a well-dressed woman with gray hair and a light complexion. She didn't look a lot like Aunt Hilda. I wondered who she was to take such an important place on the mantel, but I didn't ask. As we spoke that afternoon, I continued to glance at the photo.

We talked for a long time that day about how to live

a life of peace and how to know when to stop holding onto painful things and let them go. My aunt spoke of mistakes that she made in her life, times when she was disobedient to God, and instances where she'd been mistreated and treated unfairly. Despite these challenges, Aunt Hilda explained how all of this pain she had to bear was just a season in her life. "The seasons come, and they go," she reminded us. The pain she felt in that season was not a determination of who she was and why she was here on Earth.

She is right: Everything in life passes. Seasons change. Bad things happen, and then they move on, and then it's not happening. We must realize, in these dark or difficult moments, this is just a season. Yes, it's a difficult season, but we don't have to embrace it. We have control over our circumstances. You can remain in your wounded state, holding onto the pain, or you can say, instead, "Yes, it happened, but I don't have to continue to live in this. I don't have to have it define me. It doesn't have to determine my future." And as my great-aunt said, you must begin to live internally, not externally.

During our conversation, I noticed my aunt glancing at me a number of times. I was not sure what she was thinking. Finally, she said to me, "You know, I can feel your presence."

She could feel the essence of my spirit, she told me. We were connected spiritually. Then she looked at the picture on her mantle, the one I had been eyeing.

"That's my mother, you know." She looked at me as if she was puzzled, like she was trying to figure something out. I looked back at her, trying to figure out what was happening. She said, "I feel my mother." She was speaking of my paternal great-grandmother, who was a prayer warrior, an intercessor. Aunt Hilda told me then, in a soft voice, "The mantle has been passed on to you."

I felt the prayers of those generations before me who had committed their lives to God and covered future generations in prayer. I had a greater understanding of my spiritual identity. It made me think about the scripture in Jeremiah 1:5 which tells us, "Before I formed you in the womb I knew you" (NIV). My divine purpose and destiny had been determined even before my birth.

I knew the depth of my spirituality came from my mother's side, but now I saw it was not only through her mother's bloodline, as I previously thought, but also through her father's bloodline as well. It was handed down to me through the generations. That day, it came through my great-aunt to me, helping me navigate the questions I had been mulling over, leading me to my purpose. Perhaps it was a divine appointment for her to sit there with me that day, exactly when I needed it, to help me understand what I have inherited and how I need to move forward into my changing life, and how we reach forward and back and guide others to their own purpose. That day, I left my great-aunt's home thinking more profoundly about identity, spirituality, connection with my creator, and my divine purpose. Aunt Hilda that day saw me much like Mohammed did years before: she saw an even greater greatness inside of me.

Return to the moment when you opened this book. What was it you wanted for yourself? What pain was bringing you to these pages? I urge you to continue the work you started here. It is not easy work, and it may seem simpler to remain in your current routines and patterns of life. You must want freedom, but you must want it more than you want to live in pain. You must want to leave the place of pain and perpetual struggle. You must want to rediscover your authentic self, the you that God purposed, and reconnect with life in meaningful ways.

You came here to learn how to unburden yourself from your pain, and as you move forward, throwing off the lies you learned to believe about yourself, you will experience lighter days. Your greatness will be revealed to you, perhaps not at all once, but over time. Are you ready to go to a place of solitude within yourself to examine your pain? Will you commit to the work, knowing it is arduous? Do you want to know the purpose in the pain?

Use this space to record your thoughts.

_____

_____

_____

_____

_____

_____

⟨∼⟩

Years ago, I couldn't understand Mohammed's words. There was greatness in me, he promised, and I held onto those words all my life. His words rang clearer as I garnered accomplishments, and my purpose became clear. The purpose of my pain has been to prepare me to be an emotional and spiritual healer and teacher, helping others to navigate through the lies and pain. Who is better equipped for this type of assignment than one who has experienced it and has conquered it? Our pain is not just something we go through "just because," just as our victory is not just about us. We will move forward in connection with others, and the ripple effects of our triumph will be felt by those around us and those who come after us. Our purpose is far-reaching, beyond what we can see.

Triumph is moving above—or soaring above—the trauma. When you face challenges in this free and triumphant state, you will still face situations that are difficult. But in the pain, you will be open, you will ask questions of it and dance with it. You can still feel a sense of peace and joy in the midst of it, knowing that the purpose will be revealed to you later, even on this side. We do not have to wait until we enter Eternity. We can know it and experience it now. As the Lord's Prayer declares in Matthew 6 and Luke 11: *Thy kingdom come; Thy will be done on earth as it is in heaven.* It is meant for us to live an abundant and peaceful life here on Earth.

Triumph is not about celebrating success in the way we usually talk about it. It is not about success in our careers, making more money, or having a beautiful home. It's the joy of achievement, the sense of victory we feel when we have overcome tribulations. When we are triumphant, we don't just enjoy our successes: We experience glorious spiritual healing and oneness with our creator.

This new season of life holds many unknowns, but I am certain of one thing: I will achieve new greatness. It will be revealed if I listen. There is more greatness to come. There is more healing. There is more light.

Before, I could not see greatness because I was

unaware of what was possible. I had to believe in Mohammed's words and let the seeds of his words grow until they were rooted in my heart and spirit. The awareness came later after I worked through the lies and the pain I was living under. I had to dance with the pain and learn to lead it where I wanted to go. My greatness comes out of my sense of purpose: I was born to minister healing.

Your greatness is inside you. I see it. Where you are is not where you will be. Commit to change and move ahead with excitement and expectation. Face the pain but also look to it for signs of your passion. Passion transforms to purpose the closer you get to freedom.

In my early days of freedom, I saw myself as an eagle. The eagle was flying high above the earth but not soaring. Now, I see the eagle soaring. I'm not sure where he is going, but he is soaring. I can feel the wind under his wings, and there's a destiny holding him aloft, high above the physical earth. This sense of abundance becomes possible once we free ourselves from our false beliefs. It reminds me again of Ephesians 3:20, which says, "Now unto him that is able to do exceeding abundantly above all that we ask or think, according to the power that worketh in us…" (ESV). Where before I saw myself fighting for power, now I know it is already within me; it was waiting for me to become one with it.

As my journey continues and the seasons of life change, I will continue my work, as you will, in revealing my authentic God-purposed self. I am detaching from my ideas about who the world says I am and will no longer operate in fear and under the bondage of lies. I am headed towards a continually renewed freedom. The fact that I don't know the destination isn't as important as it once was to me. There is hope, expectancy, intention, and awareness to accompany me on this pilgrimage. There is something ahead of me that will bring forth more healing, freedom, and peace.

There is something ahead of you, too, and it will bring you triumph. Face the pain, dance with it, learn from it, and use it to uncover your purpose in life. You, too, can soar above the pain. Your best days are ahead of you. You must stand in that truth.

Soaring Above

A majestic bird, with wings unfurled,
Climb the winds above the world.
Eagle soars in skies so vast,
A symbol of freedom, unsurpassed.
With eyes that pierce the distant blue,
it sees the world from the point of view
of where mountains bow, and rivers weave,
a tapestry that the heavens conceive.
It writes its tale in graceful arcs:
On the canvas of the sky, so pale.
Each stroke is a testament to its might,
a dance with the clouds bathed in light.
The spirit of the eagle, wild and free,
 Speaks to the soul of what we can be.
Unbound by chains, it claims the skies,
Where dreams take wing and hope never dies.
So, let us learn from this regal flight.
To rise above, to seek the light.
For in our hearts, the eagle soars,
And in its shadow, our spirit roars.

ACKNOWLEDGMENTS

I would like to thank my eldest sister Patricia and my niece Lisa for allowing me to share a very intimate and personal aspect of their lives as mother and daughter. It is a testament of your healing and the innate Godly bond between mother and daughter despite worldly circumstances.

I am grateful for the divine introduction to Dinah Laprairie, a woman who lives thousands of miles away in Canada and whose only interaction with me has been via Zoom. It was through your coaching and encouragement that a dream deferred for over ten years became reality. We will forever be connected.

I would be remiss if I did not acknowledge Carolyn Forché who spoke words of life over me when I was in my twenties. At the time, I was lacking confidence and unsure of the possibilities that the future held for me. She saw God in me when I was blinded to it. Thank you, Carolyn.

Last but not least, it is with a heart of gratitude and love that I want to express my thanks to my husband Robert (Bobby) and daughter Rosalyn for allowing me to be me as I traveled this road of healing during many of the most challenging and painful times in my life, even before I knew healing and freedom was possible.

ABOUT THE AUTHOR

Dr. Karen Roland Douglass is the youngest of four children who were raised by their mother on the West Side of Chicago. She was a pensive and introspective child, which led her to her life's careers and her divine purpose and calling. She has been married to Robert Joseph Douglass for forty-two years and has an adult daughter, Rosalyn Camille.

Dr. Douglass has dedicated her life to serving children and families. She has worked in the social service/mental health field for over forty years, holding key leadership positions in both the public and private sectors. Dr. Douglass received her doctorate in clinical psychology from Adler University in 2002 and a master's degree in psychopharmacology from the Chicago School of Professional Psychology in 2020. She is a Licensed Clinical Psychologist in Illinois, Indiana, Arizona, and California. Dr. Douglass recently retired as a tenured psychology professor from City Colleges of Chicago; she also served as the Director of Kennedy King College Wellness Center.

She is the founder of Gilead Heals Ministries and CEO of Gilead Behavioral Health, P.C., a small community mental health clinic in the Chatham-Avalon, a once prominent African American community on the south-side of Chicago. Dr. Douglass travels nationally and internationally to raise awareness about spirituality and mental health. She has been a member of and passion-ately serves at her local church-Apostolic Faith Church under the leadership of Bishop Horce E. Smith, MD and First Lady Susan Davenport Smith for forty-four years. Dr. Douglass is actively involved with Pentecostal Assemblies of the World's (PAW's) International Way-farers Auxiliary, the Committee on Health, Education and Wellness (CHEW), and the Department of Trans-formational Leadership.

Dr. Douglass describes herself as an emotional and spiritual healer and her life's mission is to be a blessing to others.